T0276956

The Long-Term International Economic Position of the United States

C. Fred Bergsten, editor

PETERSON INSTITUTE FOR INTERNATIONAL ECONOMICS
WASHINGTON, DC
MAY 2009

C. Fred Bergsten has been director of the Peterson Institute for International Economics since its creation in 1981. He was the most widely quoted think tank economist in the world over the eight-year period 1997–2005. He testifies frequently before Congress and appears often on television. Dr. Bergsten was assistant secretary for international affairs of the US Treasury (1977–81); undersecretary for monetary affairs (1980–81), representing the United States on the G-5 Deputies and in preparing G-7 summits; assistant for international economic affairs to Dr. Henry Kissinger at the National Security Council (1969–71); and senior fellow at the Brookings Institution (1972–76), the Carnegie Endowment for International Peace (1981), and the Council on Foreign Relations (1967–68). He was chairman of the Competitiveness Policy Council, which was created by Congress, throughout its existence from 1991 to 1995; and chairman of the APEC Eminent Persons Group throughout its existence from 1993 to 1995.

This is the fortieth book that he has authored, coauthored, or edited. The latest include *China's Rise: Challenges and Opportunities* (2008), *China: The Balance Sheet—What the World Needs to Know Now about the Emerging Superpower* (2006), *The United States and the World Economy: Foreign Economic Policy for the Next Decade* (2005), and *The Dilemmas of the Dollar* (2d ed., 1996).

Dr. Bergsten has received the Meritorious Honor Award of the Department of State (1965), the Exceptional Service Award of the Treasury Department (1981), and the Legion d'Honneur from the Government of France (1985). He has been named an honorary fellow of the Chinese Academy of Social Sciences (1997). He received MA, MALD, and PhD degrees from the Fletcher School of Law and Diplomacy and a BA magna cum laude and honorary Doctor of Humane Letters from Central Methodist University.

PETER G. PETERSON INSTITUTE
FOR INTERNATIONAL ECONOMICS
1750 Massachusetts Avenue, NW
Washington, DC 20036-1903
(202) 328-9000   FAX: (202) 659-3225
www.petersoninstitute.org

C. Fred Bergsten, *Director*
Edward A. Tureen, *Director of Publications, Marketing, and Web Development*

Copyediting by Madona Devasahayam
Typesetting by Susann Luetjen
Printing by United Book Press, Inc.

Printed in the United States of America

12   5 4 3 2

Library of Congress Cataloging-in-Publication Data

The long-term international economic position of the United States / C. Fred Bergsten, editor.
    p. cm.
    Includes bibliographical references and index.
    ISBN 978-0-88132-432-7
    1. Budget deficits--United States. 2. Debts, External--United States. 3. Fiscal policy--United States. 4. International economic relations--21st century. I. Bergsten, C. Fred, 1941- II. Peterson Institute for International Economics.
    HJ2052.L66 2009
    336.3'4350973--dc22
                                    2009015444

Contents

Preface

The current account and net international investment position of the United States, and their impact on the world economy, have been central issues on the research agenda of the Peterson Institute for International Economics throughout its history since 1981. Some of our most important studies on that topic have been prepared by authors of chapters in this volume, including Catherine L. Mann's *Is the US Trade Deficit Sustainable?* in 1999 and William R. Cline's *The United States as a Debtor Nation* in 2005. Our colleague John Williamson and I organized, and edited the results of, two major conferences on the exchange rate component of the issue in 2003 (*Dollar Overvaluation and the World Economy*) and 2004 (*Dollar Adjustment: How Far? Against What?*).

This Special Report looks at the long-run prospects for the international economic position of the United States, with particular focus on the likely evolution of the current account deficit and prospective foreign financing for it. Its goal is to provide a fundamental framework for the development of US fiscal and other economic policies, especially including responses to the current financial and economic crisis. The central message is that the long-run outlook is extremely worrisome, under plausible assumptions concerning the likely path of the US and world economies, and that policy both in this country and abroad (since "it takes two to tango") should thus aim to sharply limit the renewed build-up of US external deficits and debt in the years ahead.

The papers in this Special Report were prepared for the initial conference hosted by the new Peter G. Peterson Foundation in New York on December 10, 2008. The conference, chaired by Mr. Peterson and David Walker, the president of the Foundation, sought to draw attention to these basic problems facing the US economy, and especially how their international dimensions are likely to evolve if left unattended, and to devise effective policy responses to them. The list of attendees at the conference can be found in appendix A to this Special Report and included former secretaries of the Treasury Paul O'Neill, Robert Rubin, and George Shultz; former chairmen of the Federal Reserve Alan Greenspan and Paul Volcker; former chairman of the Council of Economic Advisers Martin Feldstein; former senator Bill Bradley; and international financier George Soros. The Peterson Foundation and the Peterson Institute are completely separate organizations.

The bottom line of this Special Report, as I have mentioned, is that the international economic position of the United States is on a trajectory that is very worrisome and potentially very costly—in foreign policy/national security as well as economic terms. As the country (and the world) emerges from the current crisis, and even in fashioning policy responses to the crisis itself, it will be essential to keep these long-run considerations firmly in mind. This will inter alia require early and decisive policy actions, perhaps even in tandem with the near-term stimulus and housing initiatives, to address the ever-escalating costs of the major entitlement programs, Social Security and especially Medicare/Medicaid, and thus the country's overall fiscal position.

The Peter G. Peterson Institute for International Economics is a private, nonprofit institution for the study and discussion of international economic policy. Its purpose is to analyze important issues in that area and to develop and communicate practical new approaches for dealing with them. The Institute is completely nonpartisan.

The Institute is funded by a highly diversified group of philanthropic foundations, private corporations, and interested individuals. About 35 percent of the Institute's resources in our latest fiscal year were provided by contributors outside the United States, including about 8 percent from Japan. The Institute prepared these analyses at the request of the Peter G. Peterson Foundation—a completely separate entity from the Peterson Institute—whose funding for the project is greatly appreciated.

The Institute's Board of Directors bears overall responsibilities for the Institute and gives general guidance and approval to its research program, including the identification of topics that are likely to become important over the medium run (one to three years) and that should be addressed by the Institute. The director, working closely with the staff and outside Advisory Committee, is responsible for the development of particular projects and makes the final decision to publish an individual study.

The Institute hopes that its studies and other activities will contribute to building a stronger foundation for international economic policy around the world. We invite readers of these publications to let us know how they think we can best accomplish this objective.

C. Fred Bergsten
Director
April 2009

Introduction

The Global Crisis and the International Economic Position of the United States

C. FRED BERGSTEN

The global financial and economic crisis is likely to change the outlook for the international economic position of the United States in several, perhaps fundamental, ways.

First, it will sharply *reduce* the current account deficit in the short run. Lower foreign growth will only partly offset the combination of US recession and much lower oil prices. In chapter 2 William R. Cline calculates that the US external imbalance could drop as low as 3.1 percent of GDP ($430 billion) in 2009. This would be its lowest level since 1998. The gains are likely to be short-lived, however, as noted below.

Second, the crisis will sharply *increase* the budget deficit. Lower tax revenues and increased spending, including for fiscal stimulus and financial rescue operations, will probably raise the US internal imbalance to at least 10 percent of GDP (about $1.4 trillion) for the next couple of years.

Third, the crisis has created an unprecedented demand for safe dollar assets and particularly US Treasury securities. The dollar has strengthened, by about 13 percent on average and about 20 percent against the euro, since the crisis entered its acute phase in early 2008 despite the central role of the United States in the turmoil. Yields on Treasuries dropped sharply, almost to zero on short-term maturities during some periods.

How do these developments affect the prospects for long-term US sustainability? We suggest answers to that question by assessing the outlook for the external and budget deficits to 2030, on sharply different assumptions regarding the latter, and then analyzing both the role of the foreign

C. Fred Bergsten has been director of the Peterson Institute for International Economics since its creation in 1981. He was assistant secretary of the Treasury for international affairs during 1977–81 and assistant for international economic affairs to the National Security Council during 1969–71.

imbalances in triggering the crisis and how the crisis itself might affect the (un)sustainability of future deficits.

Recent developments further demolish the simplistic version of the "twin deficits" thesis—i.e., a rise (decline) in the budget deficit necessarily produces a rise (decline) in the external deficit. Moreover, we do not know how private saving will respond to the unfolding of the crisis and recovery from it; the rapid rise in housing and equity wealth presumably had a great deal to do with the precipitous fall in private saving in recent years, so that variable could rebound substantially with the sharply negative wealth impact of the crisis. In light of the huge uncertainties surrounding the amount (and even the sign) of any changes in private saving, however, and the inability to date of the United States to devise policy tools that would reliably alter it, we stress the fiscal position as a key driver of the external accounts and the primary policy instrument for affecting them.[1]

The Long-Run Prospects

In chapter 2 Cline first calculates a "benign baseline" scenario premised on an early return to a fiscal deficit of only 2 percent of GDP, maintained through 2030. Even on that highly optimistic budget prospect, the net international investment position of the United States (its "net foreign debt") would climb steadily from its present 30 percent of GDP to about 70 percent by 2030. This substantially exceeds the generally accepted prudential threshold of 40 to 50 percent, and there is evidence that net foreign debt at such a level could push up US interest rates as the appeal of dollar assets to foreigners is reduced. The current account deficit remains at 4 to 5 percent of GDP, which many analysts would see as beginning to test the limits of sustainability for external financing. Nonetheless, US "debt service" remains positive until 2020 and is minimally negative thereafter despite the growing "net debtor" position because the return on foreign assets held by Americans is so much higher than the return on US assets held by foreigners.

Cline's benign baseline is only slightly more pessimistic than the "current law" baseline calculated by the Congressional Budget Office (CBO). By statute, that calculation assumes no change in tax law, even though partial replacement of the 2001 and 2003 tax cuts when they expire in 2010 is likely, as is some relief from the alternative minimum tax. The current law baseline also assumes no increase in real discretionary spending (and hence a persistent decline of this spending as a percent of GDP).

It has accordingly become CBO practice to include an "alternative sce-

---

1. The external imbalance, of course, equals the difference between national (public and private) saving and total investment in the economy. An external deficit can be reduced only through some combination of lower investment, higher private saving, and/or higher public saving (a stronger budget position).

nario" meant to reflect current policy trends. Under that scenario, which was more realistic even before the crisis and is now much more so, the fiscal deficit rises to 10 percent of GDP by 2030. The current account imbalance would then climb to 15 to 25 percent of GDP (figure 2.3 in chapter 2) and net US foreign debt would hit 140 to 175 percent of GDP—far above any levels that could be considered "sustainable." The key transmission mechanism would be a renewed rise of about 20 percent in the trade-weighted value of the dollar, promoted by interest rates about 240 basis points higher (7.4 percent instead of 5 percent) than in the baseline. The recent sharp rise in the budget deficit and strengthening of the dollar due to the crisis, which will increase the external deficit after its present temporary improvement, may have already begun this process. Cline concludes that there would likely be a run on the dollar and "some form of crisis" long before these extreme numbers could eventuate.

On this "fiscal erosion" scenario, Cline shows that the United States would be transferring almost 7 percent of its GDP abroad annually by 2030 to service its huge net international debt position (despite continuing higher returns to US investors). In addition, the inevitable adjustment in the current account position would force Americans at some point to curb domestic demand by at least 13 percent of GDP annually—a huge number perhaps double the maximum hit that is likely from the current crisis, severe as that is likely to be. Although the recent rebound in household saving from zero to about 5 percent of disposable income (or 3.5 percent of GDP) could partially offset the adverse effect of fiscal erosion, a considerable portion of increased personal saving could in turn be offset by a reduction in corporate profits and corporate saving from their unusually high levels in recent years (see chapter 2, figure 2.2).

In chapter 3, Catherine L. Mann analyzes the prospects for external financing of the US current account deficit. She assesses both the ability of the United States to finance its accumulating foreign debt and, more importantly, the willingness of foreigners to buy US assets. She includes both the stock and flow dimensions of the US and foreign positions, for the latter comparing the share of dollar holdings in foreigners' portfolios from both the stock and flow perspectives.

Her analysis, drawing importantly on research at the Federal Reserve Board as well as her own, suggests that a key reason for the dollar's decline of about 25 percent during 2002–08 was that foreign investors would have had to allocate more than 100 percent of the total increase in their international portfolios to US assets to finance the US external deficits of that period without any change in exchange rates and interest rates. It is also true, however, that those same foreign investors remain substantially underweighted in US assets compared with global market capitalization and other indicators of a "normal" international distribution of their holdings.

Mann applies this framework to Cline's alternative projections of future US external financial needs. Working with an earlier version of the projections, she concludes that funding for the baseline scenario of modest current account deficits (3 to 4 percent of GDP) should be readily available while the "fiscal erosion" scenario would require foreigners to continually invest 65 to 85 percent of their additional international investments in dollar assets. This would amount to a huge shift from "home bias" to "US asset bias" and starts to "look unreasonable!" Mann emphasizes that it is not so much the average investment required of foreigners but rather the marginal demand on their investable wealth that drives the unsustainability of the US external deficit from the financial standpoint. Moreover, the updated projections in chapter 2, taking account of the now stronger dollar, indicate even more pessimistic trajectories for both scenarios.[2]

Even before the current crisis, the likely evolution of the US external economic position thus appeared highly vulnerable unless the budget deficit could be corrected to much lower levels or private saving could increase by similarly large amounts. The crisis has sharply raised the starting point for the fiscal imbalance and thus, despite the temporary improvement it will generate in the current account deficit, increases the future risks via the international sector. This element of the equation clearly increases the urgency of launching remedial fiscal action as soon as the short-term outlook improves enough to do so.

Implications of the Current Crisis

The current global financial and economic crisis has other important implications for the US external position as well. Many observers believe that the crisis was at least partly caused by the large and persistent international imbalances. The sizable US current account deficits, which exceeded 6 percent of GDP at their peak in 2006, required net capital inflows of identical magnitudes from the rest of the world. These inflows lowered US interest rates, by 50 basis points or more according to various estimates, and permitted monetary policy to remain much easier than otherwise. This in turn facilitated the credit bubble and the excessive leveraging of the financial system, centered on housing but radiating much more widely, that burst in 2007–08 and brought on the crisis.

The external imbalances and related capital inflows did not, of course, *force* the United States to adopt an excessively easy monetary policy and inadequate regulation of its financial markets, and thus to experience a credit bubble. It could have chosen alternative policy courses that would have prevented at least the worst of the financial excesses and thus the

2. In chapter 2, current account deficits through 2030 are in a range of 4 to 5 percent of GDP instead of 3 to 4 percent in the benign baseline. In the fiscal erosion scenario, the current account deficit reaches 7.5 percent of GDP in 2020 and 15.9 percent in 2030, instead of the 6.9 and 14.7 percent levels reached respectively in the earlier projections used in chapter 3.

severity of the current turmoil. But the ready availability of huge amounts of foreign financing facilitated lending into new (and clearly dangerous) territory and ready opportunities for the increased leveraging that magnified both the buildup of all kinds of debt and the repercussions that are now being felt so widely and so deeply.

There are at least two major paradoxes, however, in the relationship between the international financial position of the United States and the current crisis. One is that the crisis occurred at least partly because the rest of the world was *too* willing to finance US current account deficits rather than becoming unwilling to do so. The classic "hard landing" scenario (Marris 1985) envisaged a "capital strike" (now often called a "sudden stop") through which foreigners stopped lending to the United States and forced a draconian contraction of the US economy. The United States has experienced instead an opposite scenario under which the external investors gave us more than enough rope to hang ourselves.[3]

The second paradox is that, at least as of this writing, the dollar strengthened rather than weakened as the crisis intensified. After declining by a trade-weighted average of about 25 percent from early 2002 through early 2008, the dollar has rebounded by about 13 percent since the spring of 2008. The move against individual key currencies has been even greater—e.g., down over 50 percent against the euro from its trough in late 2000 and then back up by about 20 percent. An increased demand for dollar liquidity and the equally weak (or even weaker) outlook for other major countries pushed up the dollar despite the continuation of large, if reduced, US external deficits and net foreign debt.

Despite these paradoxes, which run counter to most prior analyses of these problems, the unfolding impact of the crisis on the US economy looks similar to the warnings of most international economists concerning the ultimate adjustments that would be forced on the United States if it continued to run large external imbalances (see a series of Institute publications from Mann 1999 through Bergsten 2005 and Cline 2005). Those forecasts envisaged a period, probably lengthy, during which US domestic demand would have to grow more slowly than total output in order to permit the current account deficit to decline to a sustainable level (perhaps 3 percent of GDP) without generating excessive inflationary pressures (e.g., Mussa 2005).

Just such an adjustment began around mid-2006. Since then, real net exports of goods and services (as recorded in the GDP accounts) have strengthened by over $200 billion, and most forecasters believe that at least

---

3. The impact of such international imbalances is not confined to the United States and its foreign creditors. The equally large imbalances within Euroland suggest that surplus Germany gave deficit Spain enough rope to hang itself via a very similar housing collapse despite a much more solid banking system.

another $50 billion to $100 billion is in the pipeline.[4] Over the four quarters through the fall of 2008, these gains in fact wholly offset the declines in domestic demand that began in late 2007.

This reverses the pattern of the previous decade, when domestic demand grew considerably faster than output with the result that the current account deficit grew from near zero in the early 1990s to over 6 percent of GDP in 2006. One important cause of the recent reduction of the trade imbalance was of course the substantial (though gradual and orderly) decline of the dollar over the previous six years. But the real adjustment, via the trade balance and the domestic slowdown, turned out to start too late and take too long to prevent the financial effects of the imbalances from helping burst the bubbles and bring on the crash.

The relationships between the crisis and the buildup of US external deficits and debt remain controversial. Some of the traditional linkages that were thought to be among the most risky have not eventuated. On the other hand, a "hard landing" is clearly occurring and the real adjustment costs now being experienced by the US economy are precisely those suggested by most long-standing fears over the unsustainability of the US external accounts.

The foreign dimension of the crisis also needs to be taken into account. Many economies large and small, including such global powers as China and Germany, found it much easier during the 2003–06 upswing to rely on booming exports to the United States and growing trade surpluses than on expanding domestic demand. Just as the United States would inevitably have to curb the growth of domestic demand to reduce its deficits, these countries would inevitably have to expand domestic demand to offset their falling external surpluses. But it remains unclear whether they will be able to do so, and the global slowdown/recession may also turn out to be much greater as a result of this additional legacy of the persistent imbalances.

A central question is thus whether the "dollar crisis" that has been predicted for the US economy for over 20 years has already arrived, albeit under a different label and following different dynamics from the traditional model. Do we believe that the US international position has played a sufficiently important causal role in bringing on the current crisis that we must resolve to avoid such a level of external imbalances in the future? If we do, could the links to the crisis provide sufficient evidence to convince the public that, as part of the wide-ranging postcrisis effort (including new financial regulation) that will undoubtedly ensue to attempt to prevent similar shocks in the future, the United States (and the rest of the world) must adopt policies to that end?

---

4. The more familiar current account deficit in nominal dollars, as opposed to real volumes, declined much less in the early part of the period because of the soaring price of oil imports but is now improving much faster as the oil price plummets (as already seen in the monthly trade numbers in late 2008 and early 2009).

In particular, could such reasoning make a major contribution to the adoption of future strategies to avoid large budget deficits, even perhaps to run modest budget surpluses during boom periods for the economy (as the United States should have continued doing in the early years of this decade), since fiscal policy is one of the few instruments available to government to increase national saving and thus curtail excessive dependence of the United States on foreign capital? Alternatively, or in addition, could these concerns spark a serious effort to discern and implement measures that could significantly increase private saving (once the economy is growing again at a sufficient pace to absorb the corresponding cutback in consumption)? The answers to all these questions will of course turn in part on how the current crisis plays out, particularly in terms of its depth and duration, and on the further understanding of its causes that will undoubtedly emerge over the coming months and years.

Several other important lessons for future policy toward the US external economic position may be derived from the current crisis.[5]

One is whether the US authorities could employ the same crisis response policies as on this occasion if the country entered the next crisis with much larger fiscal and external deficits. The extension of massive federal loans and guarantees for financial (and some nonfinancial) firms, large cuts in interest rates, and substantial fiscal stimulus measures have been possible (at least so far) because the world retains confidence in US government debt and in the financial commitments of the US government and the Federal Reserve. Such actions might not be possible if the United States enters a future crisis with much greater internal and external imbalances, at least without driving up interest rates and risking a disorderly run on the dollar. The room for maneuver in managing the next crisis might be considerably smaller.

This would be particularly true if the Europeans (or anybody else) were to offer a more credible alternative by the time the next big crisis hits. If the euro and European financial paper were widely viewed as more attractive than the dollar or Treasury securities, it would clearly be harder for the US authorities to rescue their own economy and the world's. Europe has not distinguished itself in this crisis, enabling the United States to deploy its policy instruments without serious competition, but that may not remain the case.[6]

Second, the crisis demonstrates that unexpected financial-sector losses can be quite large and hence add to potential long-run demands on the

---

5. Peterson Institute Senior Fellows Morris Goldstein and Michael Mussa contributed substantially to this section of the chapter.

6. The crisis in fact represents a major stress test for Euroland, to see whether a currency union can survive without a common fiscal policy or regulatory apparatus, but has also greatly enhanced its appeal to nonmembers who want to get inside its perimeter of stability.

budget. This adds further to the imperative of controlling fiscal policy in the period ahead.

Third, the crisis has stained the reputations of US financial firms and US regulators and indeed of the "American model of capitalism" and of the United States as a whole. Many foreign as well as domestic investors no longer believe that US financial markets are the "gold standard" they previously thought, and broader foreign policy and even national security questions have been raised as well. In chapter 4, Adam S. Posen particularly draws implications for the international role of the dollar and how that in turn may affect America's broader reputation, credibility, and power positions in world affairs, concluding that continued significant deterioration in its external economic position would considerably undermine the global "soft power" of the United States.

However, it is far too early to assess the seriousness of this risk and, as noted above and by Posen, there is little evidence to substantiate it to date. But any movement in that direction would highlight the risks for the United States of trying to finance future external imbalances and could bring even more serious if intangible costs for the United States.

Fourth, other countries will also be drawing lessons from the crisis to guide their future policies. In particular, emerging-market economies (and others that manage their exchange rates) will almost certainly aim to self-insure through even larger accumulations of reserves than we have witnessed in recent years. China's hoard of $2 trillion will now look especially attractive to others who have seen sudden large declines in their reserves as they defended their currencies against sharp falls. For example, some India experts (Subramanian 2009) have suggested that India alone might target a level of $1 trillion (compared with its recent peak of $315 billion, previously regarded by most Indians as far too high) to protect itself in the future. Such a new mercantilist competition would of course include deliberate currency undervaluations, perhaps of substantial magnitudes à la China in recent years, which would (again) promote dollar overvaluation and increase the likelihood that the United States would (again) run large current account deficits with all the corresponding perils discussed here unless it takes strong and explicit countervailing actions.

Conclusion

Whether we view the current crisis as largely or only partially caused by the US external imbalances and their foreign counterparts, and whether we view the "benign baseline" or at least some measure of the "fiscal erosion" scenario as a more accurate projection of the future budget position and thus the current account deficit, it is clear that those imbalances pose serious risks for the United States and indeed for the world economy as a whole. The risks range from moderate to catastrophic but they clearly exist under any reasonable expectations and tend toward the more worrisome end of the spectrum on a sober judgment concerning the fiscal outlook.

There is thus a very strong case for initiating, and maintaining, preventive policies that will limit the external imbalances of the United States to a modest (perhaps 3 percent) share of GDP. This could be achieved by running the economy at subpar growth rates on a continuing basis but that is obviously undesirable. Partial relief could come from higher private saving (and a correspondingly weaker exchange rate for the dollar), but there is no firm basis for anticipating either an autonomous and lasting rise of significant magnitude or policy steps that could reliably promote such an outcome. The only prudent alternative is to run a responsible fiscal policy, including at least modest surpluses during periods of above-normal growth. In addition, more effective international rules and multilateral arrangements are needed to prevent prolonged and substantial currency undervaluations by other major trading countries. The United States and the rest of the world clearly need to broaden their responses to the current crisis, and especially their long-term strategic planning, to reduce the probability of the recurrence of even more severe crises in the foreseeable future.

References

Bergsten, C. Fred, and the Institute for International Economics. 2005. *The United States and the World Economy: Foreign Economic Policy for the Next Decade*. Washington: Institute for International Economics.

Cline, William R. 2005. *The United States as a Debtor Nation*. Washington: Institute for International Economics and Center for Global Development.

Mann, Catherine L. 1999. *Is the US Trade Deficit Sustainable?* Washington: Institute for International Economics.

Marris, Stephen. 1985. *Deficits and the Dollar: The World Economy at Risk*. Washington: Institute for International Economics.

Mussa, Michael. 2005. Sustaining Global Growth while Reducing External Imbalances. In *The United States and the World Economy: Foreign Economic Policy for the Next Decade*, C. Fred Bergsten and the Institute for International Economics. Washington: Institute for International Economics.

Subramanian, Arvind. 2009. Preventing and Responding to the Crisis of 2018. *Economic and Political Weekly* (January 10). Available at www.epw.org.in.

2

Long-Term Fiscal Imbalances, US External Liabilities, and Future Living Standards

WILLIAM R. CLINE

The long-term economic challenges facing the United States include the need to avoid widening, unsustainable fiscal and external deficits as well as to rebuild private saving from its extremely low levels of recent years. This chapter first examines the long-term outlook for the US current account balance and net international liabilities under a "benign" fiscal scenario that implies considerable future fiscal adjustment. It then considers the consequences for the US external sector if instead fiscal accounts are allowed to deteriorate sharply in future decades in the face of rising social spending.

Long-Term Current Account Baseline

In Cline (2005) I set forth a model of the US current account balance that incorporates the response of trade to the real exchange rate and to economic activity in the United States and abroad and includes capital service earnings and payments that depend on US foreign assets and liabilities.[1] In that study, the long-term baseline for the current account identified a

William R. Cline, senior fellow, has been associated with the Peterson Institute for International Economics since its inception in 1981 and holds a joint appointment at the Center for Global Development.

1. In the preferred Krugman-Gagnon Symmetrical (KGS) model of that study, income elasticities are set at 1.5 on both the import and export sides. Similarly there are symmetrical elasticities of 2 for cyclical changes in growth. Instead of applying a higher income elasticity for imports than for exports (the Houthakker-Magee assumption), the secular upward drift of imports relative to exports is captured by application of symmetrical export and import elasticities with respect to capacity growth (0.75 on both sides), combined with a higher trend capacity growth rate abroad than in the United States.

widening deficit that would have risen from 5.7 percent of GDP in 2004 to 14 percent by 2024. The corresponding path for net foreign liabilities would have been an increase from 22 percent of GDP in 2004 to 135 percent of GDP in 2024. The strong implication was that the current account was on an unsustainable path, even though by the first half of 2005 the dollar had already fallen about 15 percent from its peak overvaluation in early 2002.

Subsequently, the United States set the stage for considerable external-sector adjustment. The real effective exchange rate of the dollar fell by an additional 11.3 percent from its level in January–May 2005 (the base of the 2005 study) to July 2008, further boosting US international competitiveness.[2] With a sharp decline in oil prices in the second half of 2008, slow growth in 2008 and recession in 2009 and hence falling imports, and strong export growth in 2008, the US current account deficit shifted to a narrowing path for the near term. The deficit had already fallen from 6.1 percent of GDP in 2006 to 5.3 percent in 2007 and eased further to 4.7 percent in 2008. However, as a consequence of the safe-haven effect in the face of the global financial crisis, the trade-weighted value of the dollar rose by about 13 percent from its trough in March 2008 to its average level in February 2009 (Federal Reserve 2009). The prospective further narrowing of the current account deficit in 2009 from lower imports associated with recession and the collapse in oil prices will likely be partially reversed by 2010 as a result of the lagged effects of the recovery in the dollar.

Table 2.1 reports projections of the US external account using the same model as applied in Cline (2005). The results for 2009 and 2010 take account of global recession followed by recovery. Private-sector consensus forecasts are the basis for the estimate of the sharp decline of US real GDP in 2009, by 2.6 percent (Blue Chip 2009). This decline would be larger than in the previous worst recession since the 1930s, that in 1982 when output fell by 1.9 percent (IMF 2008b). The outlook in 2009 is for a major further reduction in the current account deficit—to 3.1 percent of GDP—mainly because of a collapse in oil prices but also as a consequence of a sharper decline in imports than exports. In 2010, lagged response to the recent loss of competitiveness of the dollar combines with some recovery in oil prices to widen the deficit once again to 4.5 percent of GDP.[3]

---

2. The Federal Reserve's broad real index for the dollar, with a base of March 1973 = 100, peaked at 113.0 in February 2002. By the first five months of 2005 it had fallen to 96.6. From then to July 2008, it fell to 85.6, close to its two all-time lows in October 1978 and July 1995 (both at about 84).

3. The foreign asset and liability values registered a substantial reduction in 2008 as a consequence of a decline of about 40 percent in both domestic and foreign equity prices. The estimates for 2009 and after assume that US and foreign equity prices return to end-2008 levels by end-2009 and that they then return to end-2007 levels by end-2012. This would be a slower rebound than in the 1980–82 recession but a more rapid return to previous peaks than in the recession of 1974–75. As measured by the S&P 500 Index, US stock prices fell by 42 percent from 1972 to 1974 and did not return to their 1972 level until 1980.

Table 2.1 US external accounts, 2007–30 (billions of dollars and percent)

Measure	2007	2008	2009	2010	2011	2015	2020	2025	2030
Exports, goods and services	1,646	1,836	1,687	1,720	1,948	2,887	4,170	6,025	8,704
Imports, goods and services	2,346	2,517	2,048	2,301	2,587	3,529	5,005	7,148	10,286
Oil	331	453	226	277	343	598	694	805	955
Trade balance, goods and services	–700	–681	–361	–581	–639	–642	–835	–1,123	–1,582
Transfers[a]	–120	–127	–125	–130	–136	–165	–208	–263	–333
Net capital income	89	135	56	60	23	26	–39	–143	–317
Current account	–731	–673	–430	–651	–752	–781	–1,082	–1,530	–2,231
Percent of GDP	–5.3	–4.7	–3.1	–4.5	–4.9	–4.2	–4.6	–5.2	–6.0
External assets	15,355	13,005	13,197	14,471	15,727	18,894	22,682	27,548	33,787
External liabilities	17,881	17,397	18,009	19,256	20,726	25,898	33,978	44,946	60,094
Net international investment position	–2,525	–4,392	–4,812	–4,785	–4,999	–7,004	–11,296	–17,398	–26,306
Percent of GDP	–18.3	–30.8	–34.3	–32.8	–32.6	–37.9	–48.3	–58.9	–70.4
Growth (percent)									
United States	2.0	1.1	–2.6	1.9	3.0	2.75	2.75	2.75	2.75
Foreign	4.2	2.0	–0.9	2.4	4.1	3.5	3.5	3.5	3.5
Real dollars/foreign currency	0.96	1.00	0.96	1.00	1.04	1.06	1.06	1.06	1.06
Bond rate (percent)	4.6	3.7	3.0	4.0	5.0	5.0	5.0	5.0	5.0
Brent–WTI price (dollars per barrel)	72	100	50	60	74	129	150	174	206

a. Includes employment income.

13

The projections assume that by 2010, as world recovery eases the safe-haven effect, the real exchange rate of the dollar declines again to the average level of 2008 and that thereafter it declines an additional 6 percent to approximately its trough in March 2008 and stabilizes at that level. The renewed improvement in competitiveness offsets an assumed rebound in oil prices, leaving the current account deficit in a steady long-term range of about 4 to 5 percent of GDP (table 2.1). Considering 2010 as an early benchmark, the baseline deficit has fallen from the 7.3 percent of GDP projected in Cline (2005) to 4.5 percent. This change primarily reflects the impact of adjustment in the value of the dollar.

The principal additional features of the projections are as follows. First, after severe recession in 2009, US growth returns to a steady rate at its potential of 2.75 percent by 2012, after recession in 2008–09 and a temporary catch-up pace in 2010–11. Second, modest inflation is assumed, with the GDP deflator rising at 2 percent annually (and only 1 percent in 2009). Third, real oil imports grow at half the GDP growth rate. Fourth, the oil price recovers substantially (to about $85 per barrel by 2012 and $130 by 2015).[4] Fifth, following global recession in 2009, US export-weighted foreign growth rebounds from 0.4 percent in 2009 to 2.4 percent in 2010 and approximately 4 percent in 2011–13, before returning to steady growth at the potential rate of 3.5 percent thereafter.[5] The moderately higher foreign than domestic long-term growth (3.5 versus 2.75 percent) weighs against the past tendency of US imports to grow more rapidly than exports for identical domestic and foreign growth rates.

Finally, the projections explicitly take account of more favorable earnings on direct investment abroad than on foreign direct investment in the United States.[6] This difference, together with the greater concentration of US foreign assets in direct investment and portfolio equity in contrast to foreign concentration of holdings of bonds and credit claims on the United States, means that the capital services balance remains more favorable than would be expected simply from a comparison of total foreign liabilities against total foreign assets. Indeed, capital income does not turn negative until 2018, and the negative amounts remain moderate thereafter. Further details on foreign assets and liabilities and capital services payments are shown in appendix table 2A.1.

---

4. Based on forecasts by the Energy Information Administration (EIA 2009).

5. Growth estimates for major foreign economies are based on IMF (2009) and Deutsche Bank (2009) as well as other private-sector forecasts.

6. Rates of return on portfolio equity (excluding price appreciation) are set at 2.2 percent for assets and liabilities (as in Cline 2005). Based on 2005–07 results, returns on direct investment are set at 12.2 percent for foreign assets and 6.9 percent for foreign liabilities. Interest rates are based on Treasury bill and bond rates, with shares at 60 and 40 percent, respectively, for US credits abroad and the reverse for US liabilities. In addition, on the basis of observed returns from 1992 to 2007, a spread of 33 basis points is added for US credits abroad and a spread of 4 basis points is subtracted for external debt liabilities.

The broad picture that emerges is that although the United States is on a more sustainable external-sector path now than it was four years ago, it remains on a path that at best tests the limits of sustainability. With the current account deficit stabilizing in the range of 4 to 5 percent of GDP, net liabilities do not spiral rapidly out of control but nonetheless rise persistently relative to GDP. Yet this relatively benign baseline does not take account of possible future escalation of fiscal deficits, as analyzed below. Even so, net international liabilities rise from about 18 percent of GDP at the end of 2007 to about 50 percent of GDP by 2020 and 70 percent by 2030. Net liabilities already surged to an estimated 31 percent of GDP at the end of 2008 because of the sharp decline in stock prices (US holdings of equities abroad are almost twice as large as foreign holdings of US stocks) and the lower dollar valuation of foreign assets given the stronger dollar at end-2008 than at end-2007.[7]

A threshold of about 40 percent of GDP has in the past been associated with a critical turning point for debt sustainability in middle-income countries (Cline 2005, 168–69; Reinhart, Rogoff, and Savastano 2003). The United States might be thought to have more room for maneuver than middle-income countries. One reason is that it tends to owe debt in its own currency and is thus not subject to the ballooning of obligations if forced depreciation occurs (on the contrary, depreciation boosts the dollar value of foreign assets). A second reason is that the return tends to be higher on its external assets than on its liabilities. As a consequence, net capital service income does not turn negative in the baseline until net international liabilities reach about 40 percent of GDP, by about 2018. Nonetheless, other considerations suggest the United States may have less room for maneuver than most countries. One factor is that the large, rich US economy is less open than most other economies in terms of the trade base relative to GDP, so any particular percent of GDP benchmark would mean substantially higher international liabilities relative to the export base than would usually be the case. A second consideration is that as the lynchpin of the international economy, the US economy is subject to adverse feedbacks from the global economy in the event of an external-sector crisis, which could complicate adjustment of the external sector.

Overall, a prudential ceiling in the range of 40 to 50 percent of GDP for net external liabilities would seem a meaningful benchmark for the United States. Baseline net international liabilities would start to exceed the lower end of this range by 2017 and the upper end by 2022. Further simulations indicate that an additional depreciation of the dollar of about 5 percent by 2011 (compared with the baseline in table 2.1) would be required to set the

---

7. The end-2008 data on assets and liabilities in table 2.1 are my estimates; official data will not be published until June 2009.

external accounts on a path that would hold net international liabilities within this target long-term range.[8]

A potential downside risk in even this relatively benign baseline is adverse feedback of a rising net international liability position to induced increases in interest rates. Figure 2.1 presents informal international evidence supporting the notion that countries with higher net external liabilities are forced to pay higher real interest rates.

A simple regression on annual observations for 1991–2007 for Australia, the United States, and Japan yields the result that an extra percent of GDP in net international liabilities is associated with an increase in the real interest rate on government long-term (10-year) bonds by 0.0265 percentage point. So the baseline increase of the US net international liability position from 18 percent in 2007 to 70 percent by 2030 (table 2.1) would boost the bond rate by about 140 basis points, or from 5 to 6.4 percent. This increase in interest paid on a large net external debt would in turn widen the current account deficit, from 6.0 percent of GDP in 2030 before taking this feedback into account to 8.0 percent. Net international liabilities by 2030 would correspondingly reach 83.7 percent of GDP rather than the 70.4 percent level identified before considering induced increases in interest rates.

In sum, despite the considerable adjustment of the dollar and some external adjustment through domestic demand slowdown (with the weak economy of 2008–09), the long-term baseline for the US external accounts remains precarious. Net international liabilities would reach about 70 to 80 percent of GDP by 2030 even under the relatively benign conditions (and in particular, relatively favorable fiscal performance). A level this high should be seen as being already beyond the outer limits of prudence for the United States. Even so, modest additional dollar correction would probably suffice to hold the long-term net liability position within the target range of 40 to 50 percent of GDP.

External-Sector Impact of Widening Fiscal Imbalances

Even the external-sector baseline of table 2.1 may be considerably too optimistic, however, because it is implicitly premised on no major changes in the magnitudes of US fiscal imbalance experienced in recent years. The actual fiscal outcome for the federal government was a deficit of 1.9 percent of GDP in fiscal 2006, 1.2 percent in fiscal 2007, and 3.2 percent in fiscal 2008 (CEA 2008, 320; CBO 2009a, 16). Holding the current account deficit to no more than about 4½ percent of GDP in 2010–25 would be consistent with ongoing fiscal deficits centered in this range, or at around 2 percent

---

8. With the real dollars per unit of foreign exchange index at 1.10 by 2011 and after, rather than 1.061 in the baseline, net international liabilities would reach 40 percent of GDP in 2020, 47 percent in 2025, and 54 percent by 2030.

Figure 2.1   Average real interest rates on government bonds and net international liabilities, Australia, United States, and Japan, 1991–2007

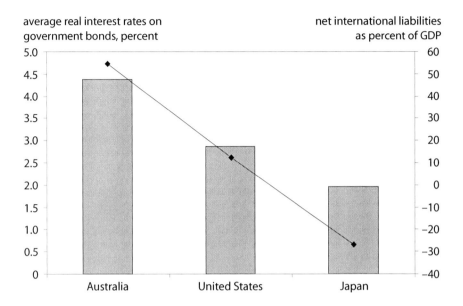

Note: The bars show average real interest rates on government bonds (left axis) and the line shows net international liabilities as percent of GDP (right axis).

of GDP. A benchmark of 2 percent of GDP will be used for the "benign baseline" estimates of this study. This range is by no means unrealistic. The average fiscal deficit for 1994–2007 was 1.3 percent of GDP (CEA 2008). A 2 percent of GDP fiscal deficit target would bring back the long-term ratio of government debt held by the public to its level of about 40 percent of GDP in recent years, after a multiyear excursion to around 60 percent as a consequence of the financial crisis and recession.[9]

Unfortunately, in the absence of major political efforts, the US fiscal deficit could easily widen to much larger magnitudes in the years ahead. It is therefore useful to examine what the baseline for the external deficit

---

9. Federal government debt held by the public at the end of 2007 was $5 trillion, or 37 percent of GDP (CEA 2008). Long-term real GDP growth for the United States is 2.5 percent per year, and inflation is 2.5 percent, so total nominal growth is 5 percent. The ratio of net debt to GDP stabilizes at the ratio of the fiscal deficit as a percent of GDP to the nominal growth rate in percentage terms, so a 2 percent benchmark for the fiscal deficit would yield a steady 40 percent of GDP ratio of net debt to GDP. In the next few years, however, federal debt held by the public could rise to 66 percent of GDP (58 percent net of financial assets) as a consequence of the financial crisis (OMB 2009, 114).

and net external liabilities would look like in the absence of meaningful fiscal adjustment measures.

The Office of Management and Budget places the fiscal 2009 federal deficit at an astounding 12.3 percent of GDP (OMB 2009, 114). In contrast, in September 2008 the Congressional Budget Office expected the 2009 deficit to reach only 3 percent of GDP (CBO 2008). By January 2009 the CBO had raised its estimate to a deficit of 8.3 percent of GDP (CBO 2009a). The change reflected greatly weakened tax revenue as a consequence of recession (2.5 percent of GDP fiscal loss) and a large expected cost of the financial crisis interventions in Fannie Mae and Freddie Mac and through the Troubled Asset Recovery Program (2.9 percent of GDP).[10] Subsequently the $780 billion fiscal stimulus program (American Recovery and Reinvestment Act of 2009) added another 1.3 percent of GDP ($185 billion) to the 2009 deficit and an additional $399 billion or 2.8 percent of GDP to the 2010 deficit (CBO 2009b). The Barack Obama administration submitted a budget proposal that added another 1.8 percent of GDP ($250 billion) as a "placeholder for … financial stabilization" (OMB 2009, 115). These successive increments, together with the effect of a smaller 2009 GDP than expected earlier, boosted the prospective fiscal deficit by 9 percentage points of GDP from the September 2008 estimate. It should be recognized that the 2009 deficit is historically unprecedented for the United States in peacetime.[11]

The new administration's proposed budget would bring the deficit back down to 8 percent of GDP in 2010, 5.9 percent in 2011, 3.5 percent in 2012, and then a steady plateau of 3.1 percent in 2013–19 (OMB 2009, 114). However, in the latter part of this period and especially in the following decade the deficit could reach far higher in the absence of painful political decisions. To consider the fiscal path out as far as 2030, it is necessary to return to the long-run budget projections of the CBO as of late 2007, its most recent analysis for this long a horizon.

The CBO remains the most authoritative source for long-term projections of US budget deficits and public debt. It is a bipartisan entity with a strong incentive to maintain its reputation for solid analysis and even-handedness, like a central bank's need to maintain its anti-inflationary reputation. There is, however, an important quirk about CBO projections. By mandate, the CBO is required to make projections under current law. A major problem arises when current law embodies unsustainable elements. In particular, under current law, the tax cuts granted under the Economic Growth and Tax Relief Reconciliation Act (EGTRRA) of 2001 and the Jobs and Growth Tax Relief Reconciliation Act (JGTRRA) of 2003 are set to

---

10. The CBO counted only the expected loss from these interventions, not their full face values, as budgetary outlays.

11. The largest previous peacetime deficit was 6 percent of GDP in 1983. The prospective 2009 deficit was exceeded only during 1942–45, when the average was 22.2 percent.

expire after 2010. Similarly, the alternative minimum tax (AMT) is part of current law, but it will increasingly sweep middle-class families into its coverage because of the absence of adjustment for inflation in its rates, and some relief is highly likely. Already its rising effective bite has routinely been deferred on an ad hoc annual basis in recent years.

The new administration's budget proposal does allow a rollback of the 2001 and 2003 tax cuts for the richest brackets, but introduces new tax cuts and credits for middle- and lower-income families and realistically accounts for reform of the AMT. As a result, it calls for revenues to stabilize at about 19 percent of GDP by 2013 and after, almost unchanged from the 2007 level instead of rising by 2.5 percent of GDP by 2030.

On the spending side, under the rules set forth in the Balanced Budget and Emergency Deficit Control Act of 1985, the baseline projections calculate discretionary spending (for defense, education, and other nonmandatory items as opposed to mandatory Social Security and health spending) under the assumption that levels remain constant in real terms rather than keeping pace with a rising GDP. So, on both the revenue and spending sides, the CBO projection rules result in an overly optimistic baseline.

The pattern of CBO projections has thus become to adhere to its current law mandate for its "baseline" projection, but then to set forth an "alternative" projection that more realistically takes account of likely changes in current law and of likely real growth in discretionary spending.[12] Table 2.2 reports the resulting estimates for 2007 and projections for 2030 in the CBO's most recent long-term projections (CBO 2007).

In the current law baseline, the rollback of the EGTRRA and JGTRRA tax cuts and the maintenance of the AMT would drive revenue substantially higher in the future, from 18.8 percent of GDP in 2007 to 21.4 percent by 2030. As a result, despite large increases in spending on Medicare-Medicaid and to a lesser extent Social Security, the fiscal deficit remains at only 1 percent of GDP by 2030. In particular, Medicare plus Medicaid rise from a combined 4.1 percent of GDP in 2007 to 8.1 percent of GDP by 2030, and spending on Social Security rises from 4.3 percent of GDP to 6.1 percent. Medical spending costs per beneficiary that rise substantially in excess of growth in per capita income are the main force in the rising health costs, rather than increasing numbers of beneficiaries. In contrast, Social Security costs increase mainly because of the demographics of more retirees.

The CBO's alternative scenario gives a much more realistic picture of the challenges that lie ahead. In this case, the unrealistic compression of

---

12. As the CBO puts it: "The 'alternative fiscal scenario' represents one interpretation of what it would mean to continue today's underlying fiscal policy.… [It] incorporates some changes in policy that are widely expected to occur and that policymakers have regularly made in the past" (CBO 2007, 2).

Table 2.2 Congressional Budget Office long-term fiscal projections: Current law baseline and alternative scenario based on present policy trends (percent of GDP)

Spending/revenue	2007	2030	
		Current law baseline	Alternative scenario
Spending	20.0	22.4	29.1
Primary	18.3	21.8	24.3
Social Security	4.3	6.1	6.1
Medicare	2.7	5.6	5.9
Medicaid	1.4	2.5	2.5
Other	9.9	7.7	9.8
Interest	1.7	0.6	4.8
Revenue	18.8	21.4	18.9
Balance	−1.2	−1.0	−10.2
Primary	0.5	−0.4	−5.4

Source: CBO (2007).

"other" (discretionary) spending in the baseline (from 9.9 percent of GDP in 2007 to 7.7 percent by 2030) is replaced by a constant-share-of-GDP assumption. As a consequence primary spending (excluding interest) rises to 24.3 percent of GDP by 2030. On the revenue side, in the alternative scenario none of the scheduled changes in the tax law is allowed to take effect, and the AMT becomes indexed for inflation. Revenue thus stays unchanged as a share of GDP (as in the new administration's proposal in 2009) rather than rising by about 2½ percentage points of GDP by 2030. With the resulting wider deficits over time and growing public debt, interest costs soar from 0.6 percent of GDP in the mandated baseline to 4.8 percent. The total fiscal deficit under the alternative scenario continuing "today's underlying fiscal policy" thus reaches 10.2 percent of GDP in 2030, rather than the minimal 1 percent in the "baseline" calculated following the CBO's projection rules.

A federal deficit of this size would be 8 percent of GDP larger than the 2 percent of GDP long-term fiscal deficit indicated earlier as consistent with the current account projections of table 2.1. For purposes of the present study, then, the benchmark for investigating the stakes in fiscal responsibility is this: Without an improvement in business as usual policy trends, the fiscal deficit will increase by 8 percentage points of GDP by 2030 from the reference "benign" level. The task for the analysis here, then, is to recalculate the prospective path of the US external accounts under the assumption that the US fiscal deficit widens by about 8 percent of GDP from the implicit deficit that underlay the initial baseline projections of table 2.1.

There is a textbook relationship between the fiscal deficit and the trade deficit that stems from national accounts identities. GDP on the product side equals consumption plus investment plus government spending plus exports minus imports. GDP on the factor payment side equals what households and firms use their income for: private consumption, private saving, and tax payments. Subtracting the second identity from the first, it turns out that the excess of imports over exports has to be equal to the excess of investment over saving (including public saving, namely the excess of tax revenue over government spending). So if a widening of the fiscal deficit reduces saving, the excess of domestic demand for resources is filled by widening of the trade deficit as additional imports fill the resource gap.

However, an extra dollar of fiscal deficit does not necessarily cause exactly one extra dollar of trade deficit. One theoretical reason is the so-called Ricardian effect. Classical economist David Ricardo suggested that if households see the government embarking on larger fiscal deficits, they will increase their private saving against the inevitable day when the government must once again collect more taxes; so there is a Ricardian offset whereby private saving goes up when public-sector saving goes down (i.e., when fiscal deficits go up). Actual experience in the past decade has flown cruelly in the face of the Ricardian hypothesis, because private saving has continued to plunge rather than rebound as the fiscal accounts shifted from sizable surplus in 1999–2000 to large deficit by 2003–05. First the stock market boom and then the now flailing housing market boom made households feel richer and thus less in need of saving; so the Ricardian view would have to argue that private saving would have fallen even more without the decline in public saving.

A more robust reason why there would be less than a one-for-one relationship between changes in the fiscal deficit and the trade deficit (despite the national accounts identity) is that indirect effects cause some offset, apart from Ricardian changes in personal saving. A wider fiscal deficit places pressure on capital markets and bids up the interest rate, and a higher interest rate discourages investment. So there will be some reduction of investment as an indirect effect of larger fiscal deficits. The result will be a smaller increase in the excess of investment over saving, and hence of imports over exports, than would have occurred if investment had remained unchanged. In the context of the contemporary US economy, moreover, higher interest rates also tend to depress consumption, because of the role of credit (and, at least until the housing bust, home equity loans) in consumer purchases.

In Cline (2005) I develop a simple general equilibrium model that seeks to incorporate these and other interrelationships. The basic insight is that three core equations must hold: Investment minus saving equals imports minus exports (national accounts identity); exports are a function of the real exchange rate (price influence) and foreign growth (income influence); and imports are a function of the real exchange rate and domestic growth. The direct and indirect effects of a wider fiscal deficit trace through these three equations in a fashion that results in a change in the external deficit, which is likely to be somewhat smaller than the change in the fiscal deficit.

In the estimates using stylized parameter values, the model finds that the change in the trade deficit is likely to be about 40 percent as large as the change in the fiscal deficit.[13] Once feedback effects are incorporated into external debt accumulation and payments of capital earnings, the ratio of the change in current account to change in the fiscal deficit is somewhat larger.

To show the impact of an 8 percent of GDP increase in the fiscal deficit by 2030 on the path of the current account, a useful approach is to identify the change in the real exchange rate that would be consistent with a resulting change in the trade balance by 0.375 x 8 percent = 3 percent of GDP. In the current account model used above, the price elasticity of exports is unity, and the pass-through of exchange rate changes to export prices is 0.8 (exporters raise their dollar prices by 2 percent when the dollar declines by 10 percent). So a 1 percent rise in the real exchange rate depresses export earnings by 0.8 percent. The model uses an import price elasticity of unity, which means that there will be no change in the dollar value of imports from a change in the exchange rate (because any change in price is just offset by change in quantity). So the trade balance change stems fully from the change in exports.

In the projections of table 2.1, exports of goods and services stand at 17.8 percent of GDP in the middle of the horizon (2020). If an 8 percent of GDP fiscal erosion is to translate into a 3 percent of GDP decline in the trade balance, amounting to a rise in exports by 3/0.178 = 16.9 percent, then the real exchange rate must rise by 16.9/0.8 = 21.1 percent. The economic force driving a rising dollar is the rise in interest rates resulting from a rising fiscal deficit, which attracts additional foreign capital and bids up the dollar.

The first change to the model projections of table 2.1, then, is to increase the real level of the dollar exchange rate by 21.1 percent (reduce the dollar cost of foreign exchange by 17.4 percent) by 2030 (or more precisely by 2028 to allow for the lag from exchange rate to outcome) from the base otherwise shown. This is done by a smooth interpolation

---

13. Thus, in an experiment with an initial fiscal shock of 3 percent of GDP, resulting in an equilibrium change of 3.2 percent of GDP in the fiscal balance, the trade balance on goods and services changes by 1.2 percent of GDP, placing the relationship at 37.5 percent (Cline 2005, 148).

of annual increments. The other necessary change is to incorporate the influence of higher interest rates on the payments of capital income. William G. Gale and Peter R. Orszag (2004) find that a 1 percent of GDP increase in the fiscal deficit leads to an increase in interest rates by 25 to 35 basis points. On this basis, the fiscal deterioration of 8 percent of GDP by 2030 is assumed here to boost interest rates by 2.4 percentage points (240 basis points) by that time, once again phased in with steady annual increments. Thus, whereas the bond rate assumed in the calculations of table 2.1 is steady at 5 percent from 2011 to 2030 (after a brief dip), in the fiscal erosion scenario the rate rises from 5 percent in 2011 to 7.4 percent by 2030. It should be noted, however, that the CBO long-term projection itself does not appear to increase the interest rate in response to the higher deficit, suggesting that its 10.2 percent of GDP fiscal deficit by 2030 in the absence of adjustment may be understated.[14]

Table 2.3 reports the results of applying an 8 percent of GDP fiscal erosion to the current account and external liability estimates in this fashion, showing the same projection variables as in the baseline case with fiscal prudence shown in table 2.1.

Comparing tables 2.1 and 2.3, and focusing attention on the outcomes for 2030, several key differences are apparent. First, exports are considerably lower in the fiscal erosion scenario, as a consequence of a stronger dollar. Second, net capital income is far more negative, at a deficit of $2.5 trillion (6.8 percent of GDP) rather than $317 billion (0.85 percent) in the fiscally prudent baseline. Third, and driving the more negative capital income result, net external liabilities are much larger in the fiscal erosion case, at 140 percent of GDP by 2030 rather than 70 percent. External assets are about $3.3 trillion smaller by 2030 than they would have been without fiscal erosion, because of an adverse exchange valuation effect from the 21.1 percent rise in the real value of the dollar. External liabilities are about $23 trillion larger, reflecting the much larger cumulative current account deficits and higher interest rates applied to larger external debt.

Will a Revival of Personal Saving Curb External Deficits?

The financial crisis and recession of 2008–09 have caused considerable expectation that the time may be at hand for a return of personal saving to more reasonable long-term levels, after its remarkable decline over the

---

14. The report is silent on the interest rate assumptions, but they can be inferred from the size of the interest bill in comparison to the size of government debt held by the public. In the current law (i.e., unrealistic) baseline, by 2030 debt stands at 10 percent of GDP and interest amounts to 0.6 percent of GDP, implying an interest rate of about 6 percent. In the "alternate" (i.e., more realistic in the absence of adjustment) scenario, debt reaches 110 percent of GDP and interest reaches 4.8 percent of GDP (CBO 2007, 4–5), implying an interest rate of 4.4 percent. This is implausibly low under such high-debt circumstances.

Table 2.3 US external accounts under fiscal erosion, 2008–30 (billions of dollars and percent)

Measure	2008	2009	2010	2011	2015	2020	2025	2030
Exports, goods and services	1,836	1,687	1,720	1,944	2,782	3,828	5,255	7,210
Imports, goods and services	2,517	2,048	2,301	2,576	3,509	4,975	7,100	10,263
Oil	453	226	277	343	598	694	805	955
Trade balance, goods and services	−681	−361	−581	−632	−727	−1,147	−1,845	−3,053
Transfers[a]	−127	−125	−130	−136	−165	−208	−263	−333
Net capital income	135	56	60	14	−72	−405	−1,129	−2,549
Current account	−673	−430	−651	−755	−964	−1,760	−3,238	−5,935
Percent of GDP	−4.7	−3.1	−4.5	−4.9	−5.2	−7.5	−11.0	−15.9
External assets	13,005	13,197	14,471	15,663	18,465	21,580	25,448	30,449
External liabilities	17,397	18,009	19,256	20,728	26,300	36,576	53,618	82,630
Net international investment position	−4,392	−4,812	−4,785	−5,065	−7,835	−14,997	−28,170	−52,181
Percent of GDP	−30.8	−34.3	−32.8	−33.1	−42.4	−64.1	−95.3	−139.6
Growth (percent)								
United States	1.1	−2.6	1.9	3.0	2.75	2.75	2.75	2.75
Foreign	2.0	−0.9	2.4	4.1	3.5	3.5	3.5	3.5
Real dollars/foreign currency	1.00	0.92	1.00	1.03	1.01	0.96	0.91	0.88
Bond rate (percent)	3.7	3.0	4.0	5.1	5.7	6.3	7.0	7.4
Brent–WTI price (dollars per barrel)	100	50	60	74	129	150	174	206

a. Includes employment income.

past several years. A corresponding possibility is that a major rebound in private saving could partially offset the long-term trend toward greater public dissaving and hence help arrest the resulting increase in the external deficit. Personal saving fell from an average of 7.3 percent of disposable income in 1986–90 to 6.0 percent in 1991–95, 3.3 percent in 1996–2000, 1.8 percent in 2001–05, and only 0.7 percent in 2006–07. Although the rate was even lower at only 0.2 percent in the first quarter of 2008, it then rose to an average of 2.3 percent for the rest of the year, and climbed further to 5 percent in January 2009 (BEA 2009).

The steady decline in the saving rate in the late 1990s and first half of the present decade was likely associated with wealth effects from price increases in households' assets, first in the dot-com stock market bubble and then in the housing market bubble. Households enjoyed rising net worth from asset appreciation and so needed less current saving to achieve net worth goals. In contrast, by end-2008, stock market losses in the United States were on the order of $7 trillion, and home equity losses, on the order of $2 trillion.[15] A rule of thumb is that the level of annual consumption declines by 4 percent of the decline in wealth (Mehra 2001). So a $9 trillion reduction in household wealth would reduce consumption by $360 billion, or about 2.5 percent of GDP and about 3.5 percent of disposable personal income. However, households are unlikely to consider these reductions as permanent and would thus scale back their consumption somewhat less.

Moreover, the same drastic conditions that may be raising personal saving are likely to reduce corporate saving. Figure 2.2 reports the path of corporate profits and personal saving over the past three decades, with both expressed as a percent of GDP (BEA 2009). In broad terms there has been a mirror image, with falling personal saving accompanied by rising corporate profits. The recent modest rebound in personal saving has similarly been accompanied by a decline in corporate profits. The implication is that to the extent the recent changes do turn out to be a watershed event reviving personal saving to higher, earlier levels, the new environment may also involve considerably lower corporate profits. The net result would tend to be little change in private-sector saving and hence little scope for offsetting prospective long-term increases in public-sector dissaving and in the rising potential path of the current account deficit.

---

15. At the end of the third quarter of 2007, households held $6.1 trillion directly in corporate equities, $5.1 trillion in mutual funds, and pension funds held $13.2 trillion. Assuming that half of the pension funds were in equities and the other half in bonds, total direct and indirect household holdings of equities were about $17 trillion. A 40 percent loss amounts to about $7 trillion. Households held $20.2 trillion in real estate assets at the end of 2007 (Federal Reserve 2008). Housing prices have fallen from their peaks by about 5 percent according to the Federal Housing Finance Agency (2008), but by as much as 22 percent from the July 2006 peak to September 2008 according to the S&P/Case-Shiller index for 20 major cities (Standard & Poor's 2008). Applying an intermediate 10 percent gives an estimate of $2 trillion for losses in housing asset values.

Figure 2.2   Corporate profits and personal saving as percent of GDP, 1980–2008

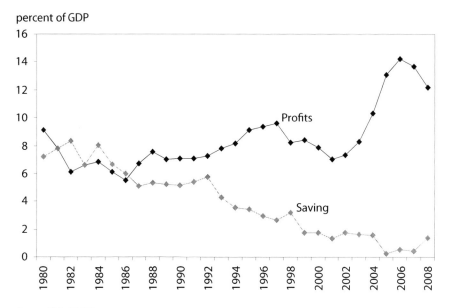

percent of GDP

Source: BEA (2009).

The Recession of 2008–09 and an Unusual Relationship of Fiscal and External Deficits

There is a major paradox in the outlook for the fiscal and external deficits in 2009. As indicated above, the current account deficit should narrow to about 3 percent of GDP, whereas the fiscal deficit could reach an extraordinary 12 percent of GDP. If the central concern of this study is that a larger fiscal deficit over time will drive a larger external deficit, how can the opposite be true in the most proximate evidence, that for 2009? The answer lies in the atypical relationship between the two deficits in a recession.

A recession tends to cause a sharp contraction in imports, as households purchase fewer imported goods. Recession can also boost exports, as firms seek to sell excess production abroad. However, recession is also a major source of fiscal erosion. As incomes fall, tax revenue declines. As unemployment rises, payments in unemployment benefits rise. The "automatic stabilizers" automatically contribute a fiscal loss during recession. So the basic expectation should be that in a recession there is likely to be a widening of the fiscal deficit and a narrowing of the current account deficit.

Nonetheless, the national accounts identity linking investment and saving to the external deficit must be met. This identity states that the trade deficit in goods and services equals the excess of domestic investment over domestic saving. Domestic saving includes both private and government saving, and government saving is defined as the fiscal surplus. The large fiscal deficit in store for 2009 does raise the question of what will be the offsetting factors that will keep the investment-saving gap from rising when government dissaving is surging.

It is useful to start from the perception that whatever government stimulus and automatic stabilizer deficits arise, they are likely at most to compensate for a collapse in private-sector demand. That is their purpose, and it is unlikely that the stimulus will be so excessive as to thrust the economy into overheating. Moreover, much of the 2009 fiscal deficit will be in the form of accounting entries that do not represent purchases of real goods and services. The bookkeeping entries for losses expected from Fannie Mae and Freddie Mac and from the Troubled Asset Recovery Program amount to 2.9 percent of GDP in the 2009 deficit, and the placeholder for further financial rescues in the administration's proposed budget adds another 1.8 percent of GDP. Thus, 4.7 percent of GDP amounts to a fiscal deficit contribution in accounting terms but not in terms of purchases of real goods and services in the national accounts.

The widening of the fiscal deficit that is germane for increased pressure on direct purchase of domestic goods and services is thus much smaller than the total 9 percent of GDP surge from the 2008 deficit (3 percent) to the 2009 deficit (12 percent). Additional layers of the increment also do not count in the national product accounts: increases in transfer payments. The influence of these transfers shows up only insofar as they induce households to spend more. Of the 1.3 percent of GDP in stimulus spending that will occur in 2009, suppose that one half is in the form of additional transfers or tax reductions. That represents an additional 0.65 percent of GDP that can be subtracted in arriving at the rise in the real government claim on production. A total of about 5.4 percent of GDP can thus be removed from the rise in the fiscal deficit to identify the extra claim on goods, reducing it from 9 percent of GDP to 3.6 percent.

This diagnosis then leaves the question of where the reduction in private demand will come from that will provide not only the supply for an extra 3.6 percent of GDP in government demand but also a reduction of 1.6 percent of GDP in external saving (the decline in the current account deficit from 4.7 percent of GDP to 3.1 percent), or a total of 5.2 percent of GDP to be accounted for. As noted earlier, personal saving is likely to rise sharply in 2009. If it were to rise from its 2008 level of 1.35 percent of GDP (BEA 2009) to its January 2009 level of 5 percent of disposable personal income, or 3.75 percent of GDP, there would be an increase of 2.4 percent of GDP in personal saving. This leaves a gap of 2.8 percent of GDP that would need to be released from net private demand. The most likely source is a plunge in investment. Business investment is expected to plunge by 13 percent in 2009 (Blue Chip 2009). Nonresidential investment was about 11 percent of GDP in 2008, so the decline would amount to about 1.4 percent of GDP. Residential investment was about 3.5 percent of GDP in 2008, and by the fourth quarter was falling at an annual rate of 23 percent. So another 0.7 percent of GDP in demand reduction could come from lower residential investment. The falling residential and nonresidential investment would largely eliminate the remaining gap in demand reduction (accounting for 2.1 percent of the 2.8 percent of GDP needed). However, as noted before, another consideration is working in the opposite direction: Corporate profits and thus business saving are also likely to fall sharply in 2009. To complicate matters further, however, about 1.6 percent of GDP, or virtually the entire amount of the reduction in the current account deficit, will come from a fall in oil prices—suggesting that there is no reduction at all in the real value of foreign saving and thus less of a puzzle to be explained in sorting through the investment-saving gaps in 2009 in the face of the megadeficit in fiscal accounts.

All will be clear when the national accounts eventually arrive, duly revised, sometime in 2010. In the meantime, the bottom line is that 2009 will be an unusual year in which there is a huge rise in the fiscal deficit but a substantial narrowing of the current account deficit. This atypical pattern should not distract attention from the long-term dynamic relevant for the fully employed economy, in which a path of ever-widening fiscal deficits if not corrected will drive a corresponding path of ever-widening current account deficits and ever-deepening international indebtedness.

Scenario Overview and Crisis Risk

Figure 2.3 shows the projections of current accounts and the net international investment position (NIIP) as a percent of GDP under four scenarios. The first (BBas) is the benign baseline of table 2.1. The second (Bas2) is that baseline after incorporation of the induced interest rate increase associated with rising net international liabilities (figure 2.1). The third (Altfisc) is the CBO alternate fiscal (fiscal erosion) case of table 2.3. The fourth (Altfisc2) incorporates the induced increase in interest rates from rising net international liabilities.

The central message of figure 2.3 is that the external accounts could be on an explosively adverse path over the next quarter century if the US fiscal deficit were to rise to 10 percent of GDP by 2030 because of uncontrolled increases in health and other social spending, as in the CBO's "alternate" long-term scenario. In the worst scenario, the current account deficit would reach 14 percent of GDP in 2025 and 24 percent in 2030. Net international liabilities would reach 109 percent of GDP in 2025 and 176 percent in 2030. Four forces drive these adverse effects. First, the rise in the

Figure 2.3   Current account and net international investment position as percent of GDP, 2007–30

a. Current account

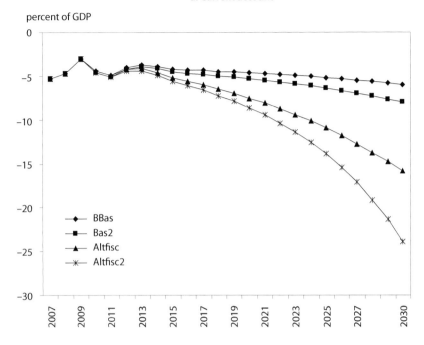

b. Net international investment position (NIIP)

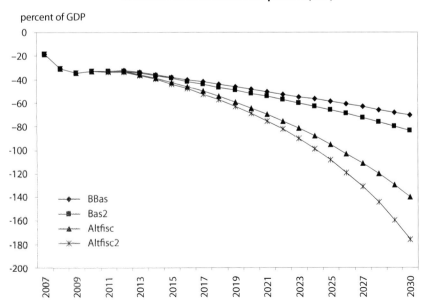

Bbas = benign baseline; Bas2 = with induced interest rate increase from falling NIIP;
Altfisc = Congressional Budget Office (CBO) alternative fiscal scenario; Altfisc2 = with NIIP-induced
interest rate effect.

fiscal deficit translates into a rise in the trade deficit that is about 40 percent as large. Second, as the real value of the dollar is buoyed up by rising interest rates and becomes the vehicle that causes the rising trade deficit, there is a reduction in the dollar value of foreign assets. Third, because of a higher interest rate associated with the rising fiscal deficit, combined with more rapidly rising net liabilities, the net capital income turns massively negative late in the horizon, instead of remaining close to balance. Fourth, further induced increases in the interest rate as a consequence of rising net international liabilities aggravate the widening external deficit and net liability positions.

Some form of crisis would be likely to disrupt the external-sector path associated with the fiscal erosion cases (Altfisc and Altfisc2) long before the current account deficit and net international liabilities reached their extreme levels of the 2025–30 projections here. There would likely be a run on the dollar, causing a sharp depreciation of the currency and forcing a narrowing of the trade deficit. With the fiscal deficit large and unchanged, other domestic absorption would have to change, probably in the form of a forced reduction of domestic consumption.

Suppose that when net international liabilities reached 80 percent of GDP (in about 2022 in Altfisc2, figure 2.3), there were such a run on the dollar. It seems likely that by that time there would have been a major shift in the currency denomination of US external debt, as foreigners became more wary of holding dollar assets. The projection numbers in the worst scenario are as follows by then: US gross external debt (bonds, banks, nonbanks) would stand at about $32 trillion and external credit claims at about $7 trillion. Suppose that two-thirds of this US external debt by then were denominated in foreign currency. Suppose that the dollar were forced to decline by 30 percent.[16] This would mean that on $22 trillion in foreign currency–denominated external debt, there would be a currency loss amounting to about $10 trillion.[17] So the dollar magnitude of foreign debt would rise to $42 trillion.

In the same scenario, US holdings of direct investment and portfolio equity abroad would amount to $16 trillion. So there would be valuation gains of about $7 trillion on these assets from the 30 percent fall in the dollar.[18] These gains would narrow the currency losses for overall net international investment from $10 trillion to $3 trillion, but these losses

---

16. For example, in the underlying model a 10 percent rise in the dollar value of foreign currency generates a 1.6 percent of GDP narrowing of the current account deficit. A forced reduction of the 2023 current account deficit from 10 percent of GDP to 3 percent would require a rise in the dollar cost of foreign currency by 7/1.6 x 10 = 44 percent, or a decline of 31 percent in the value of the dollar.

17. Or 44 percent applied to $23 billion.

18. That is: $16 trillion x (1/0.7) – $16 trillion.

would still be relatively large (at about 12 percent of GDP in 2022).[19] The United States would not yet be in the position of many developing countries that experience sharp increases in net international debt as a percent of GDP when they depreciate because their entire external debt is in foreign currency, but it would be well along that path.

Further Implications for Vulnerability and Living Standards

The overall result of the fiscal erosion scenario for the next quarter century would be to raise US external-sector vulnerability substantially by boosting the long-term current account deficit from about 4½ percent of GDP in 2020 and 6 percent in 2030 to about 16 to 24 percent by 2030, and by raising net external liabilities from 70 percent of GDP in 2030 to about 140 to 175 percent. Considering that 40 to 50 percent is a key threshold range beyond which international experience and unique features of the US economy suggest it could be dangerous to venture, even the benign baseline would arguably exceed prudential limits. Modest further dollar correction beyond that assumed in this baseline would probably suffice to keep net international liabilities within this range under the benign fiscal baseline. However, under the fiscal erosion baseline, net liabilities would go so far beyond this range as to invite crisis.

Even if there were no external-sector crisis as a consequence of rising net external liabilities between now and 2030, there would be important implications for future living standards as an increasing share of US national income would be transferred abroad to service the higher foreign debt. Comparing table 2.3 with table 2.1, by 2030 annual net payments of capital income to foreign investors would amount to 6.8 percent of GDP in the fiscal erosion scenario instead of only 0.85 percent in the fiscally prudent baseline. In addition, it is highly likely that with the net international liabilities at well over 100 percent of GDP, foreign investors would begin to insist that US external imbalances be reduced. The current account deficit would have to be cut back from about 16 percent of GDP to about 3 percent of GDP to be consistent with stabilizing the ratio of net foreign liabilities at 60 percent of GDP.[20] This would require resources amounting to 13 percent of GDP annually.

Thus, by 2030 US households would be paying about 6 percent of

---

19. Note that the scenarios shown in figure 2.3 instead assume that US external debt remains denominated in dollars.

20. This ratio eventually stabilizes at the ratio of the current account deficit as a percent of GDP to the nominal growth rate of GDP. With potential growth at 2.75 percent and inflation at about 2 percent, the nominal growth rate would be about 5 percent, and 60 percent of that would be a 3 percent of GDP limit for the current account deficit.

GDP more in capital income to foreigners than if fiscal prudence had been pursued, and in addition they would be faced with cutting back consumption by about 13 percent of GDP in comparison to the excessive levels to which they would have become accustomed. If the resources secured from abroad had been invested, then national output might have been correspondingly higher. But the resources from abroad would instead have been used for larger government spending on current consumption. Indeed, as most analyses of long-term fiscal issues conclude, the rising fiscal imbalances would reduce investment, not increase it, by raising interest rates.

These estimates for the external sector confirm the broader diagnosis that unless corrected, widening fiscal deficits will place a burden on US households by the 2020s and after. The estimates here suggest that by 2030 households could be forced to cut back consumption on the order of 19 percent of GDP (6 percent for higher capital income payments abroad plus 13 percent to trim back to sustainable current account deficits) from levels to which they had become accustomed under the fiscal erosion scenario, in comparison with the outcome under fiscal prudence.

In sum, external considerations reinforce the numerous domestic economic reasons for forceful action to prevent likely fiscal erosion over the next two decades. Rising net international liabilities could make the US economy vulnerable to an external-sector crisis, and even if no such crisis arises, excessive reliance on foreign resources would set up US households for a wrenching cutback in standards of living to which they had become accustomed once unsustainable foreign deficits were forced to be cut back.

References

BEA (Bureau of Economic Analysis). 2008. *U.S. Net International Investment Position at Yearend 2007* (June). Washington.

BEA (Bureau of Economic Analysis). 2009. *National Income and Product Accounts* (March). Washington.

Blue Chip. 2009. *Blue Chip Economic Indicators* 34, no. 3 (March 10). New York: Aspen Publishers.

CBO (Congressional Budget Office). 2007. *The Long-Term Budget Outlook* (December). Washington.

CBO (Congressional Budget Office). 2008. *The Budget and Economic Outlook: An Update* (September). Washington.

CBO (Congressional Budget Office). 2009a. *The Budget and Economic Outlook: Fiscal Years 2009 to 2019* (January). Washington.

CBO (Congressional Budget Office). 2009b. Letter to Senator Grassley on ARRA Effects, March 2. Washington.

CEA (Council of Economic Advisers). 2008. *Economic Report of the President* (February). Washington.

Cline, William R. 2005. *The United States as a Debtor Nation*. Washington: Institute for International Economics and Center for Global Development.

Deutsche Bank. 2009. Country Infobase. Deutsche Bank Research (March). Frankfurt. Available at www.dbresearch.de.

EIA (Energy Information Administration). 2009. Forecasts and Analyses. Washington: Department of Energy. Available at www.eia.doe.gov.

Federal Housing Finance Agency. 2008. Home Prices Slide Further in Summer Months: Few States Show Price Gains. News Release, November 25. Washington.

Federal Reserve. 2008. *Flow of Funds Accounts of the United States* (September). Washington.

Federal Reserve. 2009. Price Adjusted Broad-Dollar Index. Washington. Available at www.federalreserve.gov.

Gale, William G., and Peter R. Orszag. 2004. The Budget Outlook: Projections and Implications. *Economists' Voice* 1, no. 2.

IMF (International Monetary Fund). 2008a. *World Economic Outlook* (April). Washington.

IMF (International Monetary Fund). 2008b. *World Economic Outlook Update* (November 6). Washington.

IMF (International Monetary Fund). 2009. *World Economic Outlook Update* (January). Washington.

Mehra, Yash P. 2001. The Wealth Effect in Empirical Life-Cycle Aggregate Consumption Equations. *Federal Reserve Bank of Richmond Economic Quarterly* (Spring).

OMB (Office of Management and Budget). 2008. *Fiscal Year 2009 Mid-Session Review* (July). Washington.

OMB (Office of Management and Budget). 2009. *A New Era of Responsibility: Renewing America's Promise* (February). Washington.

Reinhart, Carmen M., Kenneth S. Rogoff, and Miguel A. Savastano. 2003. Debt Intolerance. *Brookings Papers on Economic Activity* (Spring), no. 1: 1–74.

Standard & Poor's. 2008. *S&P/Case-Shiller Home Price Indices*. New York: McGraw-Hill.

Appendix 2A

Table 2A.1   Additional projection details, benign baseline, 2007–30 (billions of dollars, indexes, and percent)

Measure	2007	2008	2009	2010	2011	2015	2020	2025	2030
Capital services balance	89	135	56	60	23	26	–39	–143	–317
Income	815	752	471	747	897	1,136	1,431	1,814	2,309
Payments	–726	–618	–415	–687	–874	–1,109	–1,470	–1,957	–2,625
Foreign assets	15,355	13,005	13,197	14,471	15,727	18,894	22,682	27,548	33,787
Direct investment	3,333	3,584	3,775	4,316	4,755	6,253	8,529	11,488	15,323
Portfolio equity	5,171	2,722	2,570	3,303	4,119	5,789	7,301	9,208	11,612
Bonds, loans	6,852	6,699	6,852	6,852	6,852	6,852	6,852	6,852	6,852
Foreign liabilities	17,881	17,397	18,009	19,256	20,726	25,898	33,978	44,946	60,094
Direct investment	2,423	2,809	3,051	3,307	3,578	4,830	6,840	9,479	12,924
Portfolio equity	2,833	1,642	1,599	1,911	2,305	3,188	4,021	5,071	6,395
Bonds, loans	12,625	12,947	13,359	14,038	14,843	17,881	23,117	30,396	40,775
Valuation changes	697	–1,372	–143	678	538	84	103	127	157
Prices	242	–912	19	189	270	84	103	127	157
Exchange rate	455	–460	–162	489	268	0	0	0	0
Treasury bill rate (6–month, percent)	4.44	1.62	0.50	2.36	3.36	3.36	3.36	3.36	3.36
Foreign direct investment return difference (percent)	6.3	6.9	5.3	5.3	5.3	5.3	5.3	5.3	5.3

International Capital Flows and the Sustainability of the US Current Account Deficit

CATHERINE L. MANN

The relationship between international capital flows and the sustainability of the US current account deficit can be viewed from two perspectives: (1) the US ability to repay and (2) the foreign willingness to buy US assets.

From the US perspective, financial sustainability is the cost of and ability (and desire) to make good on previously incurred liabilities—that is, given the magnitude and composition of US liabilities on the one hand and the US holdings of foreign assets on the other, how large is the ensuing net claim on US resources? Once that claim gets "too large," the ability or willingness of the United States to repay is called into question, and international capital will not continue to flow to the United States to finance the current account deficit. At that point, the US current account deficit has, by definition, become financially unsustainable.

"Too large" has both stock and flow dimensions. The stock dimension can be measured as the stock of liabilities as a share of GDP or of wealth, for example. The flow dimension can be measured as interest payments as a share of national income or as a share of exports, for example. An intermediate measure, contributing to both stock and flow dimensions, is the current account as a share of GDP. "Too large" by one dimension need not imply "too large" by another dimension, which makes it difficult to use data to determine the sustainable external position from the US perspective.

From the foreign perspective, financial sustainability is the rate of return on and desire to buy additional claims on the United States—that

Catherine L. Mann, senior fellow at the Peterson Institute for International Economics since 1997, is a professor of economics at Brandeis University.

is, given the magnitude and composition of the foreign wealth portfolio, does the foreign investor want to continue to buy equity, bonds, and ownership positions in US corporations? If the foreign investor is unwilling to continue to purchase US assets at current terms (including interest rate and exchange value), then the US current account deficit has, by definition, become financially unsustainable.

For the foreign perspective too, financial sustainability has both stock and flow dimensions. The stock dimension can be measured as the share of US assets in the value of the overall foreign portfolio of wealth. The flow dimension can be measured as the purchase of US assets as a share of the change in the value of foreign wealth, for example. Once again, sustainability as measured by stock versus flow could differ, which makes it difficult to use data to define sustainable international capital flows from the foreign perspective.

Of course, these two perspectives, and the measures of sustainability, are related. If the foreign investor calculates that the United States is less willing or able to make good on (that is, repay) previously incurred liabilities, that foreign investor is unlikely to buy more US assets (indeed perhaps will sell some) and may demand a risk premium on new claims. This risk premium makes it more costly for the United States to make good on its obligations. The presence of a risk premium in the data could be another indicator of financial unsustainability.

On the other hand, if the foreign investor does choose to sell US assets, the dollar may depreciate. To the extent that US assets held by foreigners are denominated in dollars, this depreciation represents a capital loss to the foreign investor (and a capital gain for the United States), which, along with the real effects of a dollar depreciation on trade flows, potentially enhances the ability of the United States to repay the remaining outstanding obligations. So a rapid depreciation of the dollar could be another indicator of financial unsustainability in the immediate term yet promote financial sustainability in the long term.

This short overview of international financial theory points to several analytical propositions and measures (e.g., benchmarks or thresholds) with regard to the sustainability of the current account deficit. Important benchmarks to assess sustainability might be the magnitude of obligations, the net financial cost of obligations, and the average and marginal shares of US assets in the foreign investor's portfolio of wealth. Evidence of a risk premium on new claims on US assets after a rapid run-up in foreign holdings may indicate future unsustainable financing of the current account deficit. More broadly, changes in asset prices (interest rates, equity prices, and exchange value of the dollar) are ways to gauge changes in the equilibrium between US ability to make good on international obligations and foreign desire to buy US assets.

Research on the sustainability issue addresses two questions. First, are there systematic patterns in the historical data that define benchmarks or thresholds for when the external imbalance is financially unsustainable? Second, which blade of the scissors—US ability to repay or foreign willingness to buy—is likely to do the cutting?

US Ability to Repay

The US current account deficit of the last 25 years has accumulated to a negative net international investment position (NIIP), on which, presumably ultimately, the country will make net investment income (NII) payments. As is well known, the NII stream remains positive (at least as revised)[1] despite the negative $2.4 trillion NIIP as of 2007. The magnitude of the NIIP as a share of GDP and the magnitude of the NII stream as a share of GDP are often seen as relevant parameters when considering the sustainability of the current account deficit.[2]

Numerical benchmarks for sustainability, however, are less obvious. Based on past experience of industrial countries with regard to when current account adjustment takes place, the NIIP/GDP ratio can range from –40 percent to +10 percent around the time of adjustment. Similarly, for the flow, NII/GDP can range from –10 percent to +1 percent around the time of current account adjustment (Bertaut, Kamin, and Thomas 2008, exhibits 7a and 7b). These very wide ranges (even the sign is not consistent) suggest that little information about sustainability thresholds can be gleaned from numerical benchmarks defined by NIIP/GDP or NII/GDP.

More consistent experience surrounds the intermediate measure of the current account as a share of GDP. Research in Mann (1999, 156) and Freund and Warnock (2007) among others implies that a current account deficit of around 4 to 5 percent of GDP for industrial countries is, on average, associated with an onset of currency depreciation and slower GDP growth, both of which tend to ameliorate the external imbalance. Therefore, the current account threshold appears to be the more stable of the measures of financial unsustainability.

Theory says that there should be a clear relationship between the current account and the NIIP, so why does this not play out in terms of empirical analysis? For the United States, there are two well-researched "mysteries" about the relationships between the current account, the NIIP, and NII streams. Looking into these mysteries helps inform as to why neither the NIIP nor the NII is a good indicator of external sustainability.

---

1. Initial data for NII have come in negative several times over the last five or so years but have always been revised positive.

2. Bertaut, Kamin, and Thomas (2008) emphasize that a technically more correct perspective (in that it matches a stock to a stock) is NIIP/total wealth. This is not the most commonly used benchmark, in part, no doubt, because of difficulties measuring and projecting total wealth. I take on this task for foreign wealth in the third section of this chapter.

First, the accumulation of past US current accounts does not sum to the net international investment position; in fact, valuation effects on the stock of assets and liabilities are quite significant so that the NIIP is much less than the sum of past current account deficits. The two panels of figure 3.1 show the magnitude and decomposition of the valuation effects for two periods—2002–04 and 2002–06—as of those periods (i.e., without subsequent data revisions). During this whole period, the real exchange value of the dollar was depreciating, which would tend to depress the value of US net liabilities. However, in addition to valuation effects from currency depreciation, those from differential asset prices and "other valuation" effects are important and in fact can dominate, as in the latter period. For the purposes of projecting sustainability of the US external imbalances based on the NIIP/GDP concept, a key challenge will be to project valuation effects.

Second, there are persistent differentials in the rate of return that the United States earns on its assets abroad compared with the return that foreigners earn on their assets in the United States (figure 3.2). The most important component of this differential relates to returns on foreign direct investment (FDI), where the United States has earned substantially more on its FDI abroad than foreigners have on their FDI in the United States. The rates of return on other US assets abroad exceed the rates of return earned by foreigners on their portfolio of US assets, but not by much. The rates of return on these other assets follow rather closely the US Treasury rate. In the course of projecting sustainability of the US external imbalances based on the NII/GDP concept, it will be necessary to project rate of return differentials—both for FDI and for other assets.

In sum, understanding the source and likely persistence of these two mysteries—the valuation effects and the favorable relative return on US FDI abroad—is key to any projection of NIIP and NII and the benchmark concepts based on them. In addition, the gross flows of assets and liabilities that underpin the net position and income streams are crucial for the second main perspective on sustainability, that of projecting foreign willingness to buy.

Measurement of the NIIP and Rates of Return

The mysteries associated with the US NIIP and NII have not gone unresearched. Advances in available data have spawned a burgeoning recent literature on measurement and valuation of assets and liabilities. This literature is crucial to evaluating whether the accumulated current account deficit yields a "too large" net international investment position, which the United States must ultimately service using financial and real resources. A few key examples from the literature and their implications for projections of the current account, NIIP, and NII are noted below. In sum, uncertainties with regard to valuation effects on the net international investment

Figure 3.1 Valuation changes in the US net international investment position, 2002–06

a. 2002 to 2004 (as of 2005)

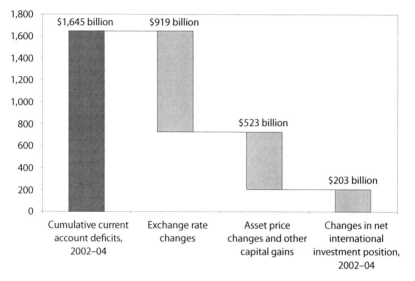

b. 2002 to 2006 (as of 2007)

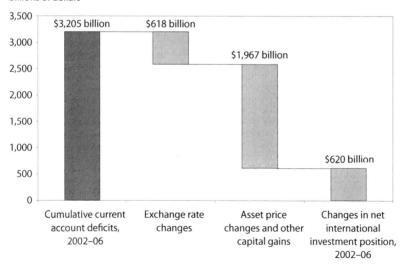

Note: Exchange rate valuation changes in 2005 came to negative $227 billion.

Source: Bureau of Economic Analysis.

Figure 3.2 Implied rates of return on US assets and liabilities, 1977–2005

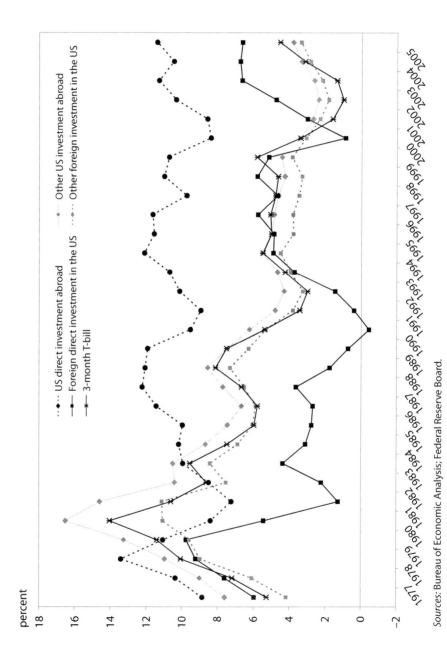

percent

Legend:
····· US direct investment abroad
⬦ Foreign direct investment in the US
✻ 3-month T-bill
Other US investment abroad
Other foreign investment in the US

Sources: Bureau of Economic Analysis; Federal Reserve Board.

position and on rates of return on assets and liabilities make projections of the future US ability to repay quite speculative.

The first issue is valuation effects. Phillip Lane and Gian Milesi-Ferretti (2007) analyze global current account and asset position data from the International Monetary Fund's coordinated survey on "external wealth of nations." They emphasize the importance of valuation effects, composed of both changes in the exchange value of the dollar and relative (US versus foreign) equity market performance. Considering just their results for the United States over the floating rate period, the relative importance of capital gains/losses due to exchange rates versus equity markets varies: Sometimes dollar valuation dominates and sometimes equity market valuation dominates. This observation can be gleaned from figure 3.1 for 2002–06.

Another analysis of the valuation effects (Curcuru, Thomas, and Warnock 2008) decomposes the valuation effects into exchange rates, return differentials, and "other," noting that the last is very large (as is also observed in figure 3.1). The authors speculate about the origin of this "other" component and wonder about its likely persistence.

Based on this research, a projection scenario cannot assume a strong or consistent relationship between dollar depreciation and valuation changes in the NIIP. First, at times, other valuation changes, including asset price differentials, swamp the effect of the dollar alone, and second, the magnitude of the currency valuation effect is not systematically related to foreign exchange movements.

The second issue is rate-of-return differentials that favor the US investor. Pierre-Olivier Gourinchas and Hélène Rey (2007) focus on the differentials in rates of return earned on US assets versus paid out on US liabilities. They develop their own dataset that generates the net international investment position "from the ground up" by recalculating gross asset and liability positions and then applying valuation adjustments to each type of financial asset. They find that the United States enjoys a net premium on its assets, which is composed of a return effect (higher returns on assets versus liabilities of similar characteristics) and a composition effect (the United States holds a riskier and therefore higher-return set of foreign financial instruments as assets compared with its liabilities, e.g., the types of US financial instruments that foreigners hold). Reduction of US home bias (i.e., preference for owning home assets), such that the US portfolio includes more foreign equity assets that have yielded a higher return, also contributes to the return premium enjoyed by US asset holders.

Differentials in the rates of return on FDI are the most important determinant of the overall return premium, as noted in figure 3.2. With regard to these return differentials, several analysts (e.g., Mann and Plück 2006, Kitchen 2007, and Higgins, Klitgaard, and Tille 2006) have documented persistent excess returns on US FDI assets relative to foreign FDI in the United States, although Katharina Plück and I (Mann and Plück 2006) note that it appears that the return differential in favor of US FDI abroad may be narrowing somewhat. The fundamentals underlying this persistent gap are not known, despite research that goes back several decades. Suggestions range from higher-quality US management to age of assets to tax differentials. Carol Bertaut, Steve Kamin, and Charles Thomas (2008) do note, however, that this asymmetry—that FDI abroad earns more than FDI in the home country—is observed for all industrial countries.

Stephanie Curcuru, Charles Thomas, and Frank Warnock (2008) analyze the non-FDI part of the return differential. They maintain, in contrast to Gourinchas and Rey (2007), that the return differentials are small. In examining the return differentials more closely, Curcuru, Tomas Dvorak, and Warnock (2007) generate their own data on portfolio debt and equity investments of US investors abroad and foreign investors in the United States based on the Treasury International Capital reporting system and benchmark surveys of holdings. They calculate that a key reason for the favorable return differential on non-FDI assets is unfavorable foreign "timing," for example, foreign investors tend to sell assets into an unfavorable market, thus worsening their holding return on US assets.

Collectively, these analyses (and simple examination of the data for the last six years) point to severe challenges to projecting the path of NIIP and NII forward. Assumptions must be made with regard to the future path of valuation effects, which are crucial to the sustainability question. Second, whereas it is common to make assumptions regarding the path for the dollar and interest rates, these analyses make clear that projections must also make assumptions on relative equity market performance and foreign investor behavior—far more difficult propositions—and also must pass judgment on "other" valuation effects and any changes in home bias. Finally, the assumption that the FDI gap will persist is crucial to the conclusion that net investment income on the net international investment position will remain small (or even positive). All these factors impact valuation effects and return differentials, which make or break conclusions with regard to the size of the NIIP, the magnitude of net investment income, and therefore the sustainability of the US current account deficit as judged from the US perspective.

Projections of US Ability to Repay

Proceeding despite the valuation and rate-of-return challenges, many who engage in a projection exercise conclude that it will be many years before the criteria of "ability to repay" is breached; in fact, sustainability probably would turn more on "willingness" to forgo domestic consumption and investment in order to service the NIIP. I reached the same conclusion in Mann (2003). Of course, each of these exercises differs somewhat. A brief summary of selected projection exercises is reported here.

The most recent scenario is by Bertaut, Kamin, and Thomas (2008), who project a negative NIIP/GDP of about 65 percent by 2020; but net investment income payment would account for only about 0.5 percent of GDP as the return differential on FDI is assumed to remain large. Similarly, John Kitchen (2007) projects NIIP/GDP rising to 39 percent of GDP with net investment income payment rising to just about 0.75 percent of GDP by the end of his projection horizon in 2016. In addition to his own scenarios, Kitchen (2007) reports on and reproduces scenarios from Higgins, Klitgaard, and Tille (2005), Cline (2005), and Roubini and Setser (2004).

As an example of the importance of assumptions regarding valuation effects and the assumption of persistently higher rates of return on US FDI abroad, Kitchen (2007) reports on exercises using the Roubini and Setser (2004) base case, which assumes that rates of return on foreign-owned assets exceed those on US-owned assets (which is opposite to historical norm) and makes no valuation adjustments (which is quite contrary to historical experience). In the Roubini-Setser "counter-to-historical-norms" projection, the negative NIIP/GDP ratio rises to more than 100 percent of GDP and the net investment income payment reaches about 6 percent of GDP. NIIP/GDP of 100 percent is well outside the bounds of industrial-country experience prior to current account adjustment. Paying 6 percent of GDP to service this negative NIIP implies draconian cuts in US domestic consumption and investment. Presumably the US ability to pay would be questioned and the external imbalance deemed financially (not to mention politically) unsustainable well before the end of their projection horizon in 2020.

However, as Kitchen notes in his version of the Roubini-Setser exercise, if the historical norm of higher US returns on FDI is applied and valuation effects consistent with historical norms are considered, the Roubini-Setser scenario plays out much the same as for the other analysts, with negative NIIP/GDP about 70 percent and net investment income payment about 2 percent of GDP by the end of the projection period.

Finally, Kitchen (2007) runs his own plausible scenario whereby the most questionable valuation effect (the "other" component) is set to zero and the FDI premium erodes to zero. In this case, NIIP/GDP reaches about 60 percent and the NII/GDP is –2.3 percent. These two comparative scenarios show the importance of these two key assumptions of FDI rates of return and valuation effects. Whereas both are important, the valuation effects appear to be the relatively more important factor that keeps the NIIP from getting "too large."

In conclusion, if valuation effects and the FDI premium are observed in the future as they have been in the past, the US-centric "ability to pay" criterion for sustainability is not likely to be the cutting blade of the scissors of sustainability. NIIP/GDP is not so large, and NII/GDP remains less than 1 percent. However, if valuation effects diminish and the FDI premium erodes, then the ability to repay hinges more on the willingness of US citizens to reduce consumption, investment, or government spending by 2 to 3 percent of GDP. While not large percentages on an individual basis, on an economywide basis these figures loom rather large given that an increase in household savings of 3 to 4 percent (just to repay international obligations) may be associated with recession[3] and/or an 11 to 17 percent shift in government spending (which is the equivalent of how much would have to be paid to foreign investors) is not in the recent US historical experience.[4]

Foreign Desire to Buy

The financing of the US current account deficit of the last 25 years, as well as the financial choices of private investors, have accumulated into the wealth portfolios of foreign investors (both private and official, inclusive of reserves, government-owned or -controlled corporations—e.g., sovereign wealth funds). So the second perspective on international capital flows as it relates to US current account sustainability is that of the global investor.

A simple overview of the international portfolio model of current account sustainability is in Mann (2002), although the underpinnings go back at least to Henderson and Rogoff (1982). How much the global investor is willing to invest in US assets is a function of the risk-return profile of the US obligations relative to financial assets of other countries, the investor's attitude toward risk and desire to diversify investments, and the overall size of the wealth portfolio.

Relatively higher rates of return or relatively lower risk are obvious determinants of portfolio choice. However, the growth of the investor's home economy, the size of his or her global portfolio, and the available supply of alternative foreign investments also are important in determining how many US assets the foreign investor might want.

Moreover, risk matters: If the variability of the rate of return on an asset increases—because of variability in interest rates, inflation rates, or exchange rates—investment in that asset generally declines, or else the asset must yield a higher return to compensate the holder for that greater risk.

There are two potential benchmarks of interest when considering the financial sustainability of the US external deficit: average and marginal. The current (i.e., average) share of US assets in the global investor's portfolio of assets is the more common measure. But the marginal investment in US assets that the global investor must make with each currency-unit increase

---

3. As indeed appears to be the case as of April 2009.

4. The increase in household savings is calculated as 2 to 3 percent times 70 percent share of consumption in GDP. The increase in the budget position is calculated as 2 to 3 percent times 17 percent share of government spending in GDP and about 50 percent share of US Treasury securities held abroad.

in wealth in order for the United States to be able to finance its ongoing current account deficit may be more important.

Key factors underpinning the global investor's choices, and therefore the desire to invest in US assets, include the overall magnitude of global wealth, its increase in size (both directly through fundamentals of GDP growth and national savings and indirectly through changes in financial leverage[5]), and any changes in investor home bias (whether by evolutionary changes in preferences or through direct changes in regulations). Clearly, it will be difficult to tie down these parameters in the context of a projection of US current account sustainability that just focuses on the United States from a stock or flow standpoint. A key challenge for this perspective on sustainability is evaluating these parameters of the foreign investor's wealth portfolio.

Size and Composition of the Foreign Portfolio

Recent research has focused on documenting the historical pattern of the share of US assets in the foreign portfolio of wealth. Home bias has been the focal point of this literature. That is, it is difficult to judge whether the US share of foreign portfolios is "too high," which might precipitate an asset sale, if we don't know what the current share is or how it has changed over time.

Lane and Milesi-Ferretti (2007), using their global financial data, measure and evaluate the share of US assets in the portfolio of global wealth. They suggest that the US share in terms of total liabilities peaked around 1999 and then fell to 2004, when their research window ends. The drop in the US equity and FDI share was particularly pronounced and accounts for the bulk of the decline in the US share in the asset holding of the global portfolio of wealth. Figure 3.3 reproduces Bertaut, Kamin, and Thomas (2008, exhibit 8), which reports that that US share in world equity market capitalization rose from about 35 percent in 1994 to about 50 percent between 1998 and 2001, before falling back to 35 percent in 2006. More modest trends, but with the same general features, are observed in the share of US bonds in world market capitalization. These observations using more recent and comprehensive data are consistent with those I reported in Mann (2003) and Mann and Plück (2006).[6] In sum, the data suggest that the US share of the global investor's portfolio now is smaller than it has been in the past, which implies that there is "room" in the portfolio for more US assets; the question then becomes, at what terms (e.g., interest rate and exchange value)?

---

5. Financial leverage is the relationship between holdings of financial assets and GDP.

6. In Mann (2003) I used the *Economist* magazine's portfolio poll, a survey of global portfolio managers, and financial data from the OECD, which were the available sources at that time.

Figure 3.3 Share of US assets in world market capitalization, 1994–2006

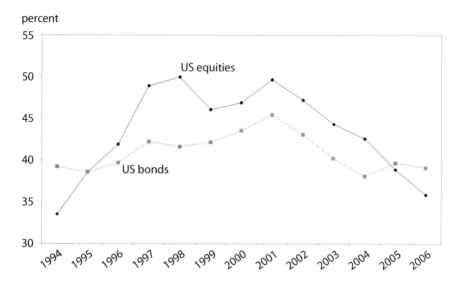

Source: Bertaut, Kamin, and Thomas (2008).

Just because the global investor is buying more foreign assets in general does not necessarily mean that he is favoring US assets. Bertaut, Kamin, and Thomas (2008) delve into their data to investigate these issues of home bias and the relative demand for US assets versus other foreign assets when the global investor chooses to buy nondomestic assets. Using the IMF's coordinated portfolio survey data and national balance sheets, Bertaut, Kamin, and Thomas calculate the US share in the global investor's[7] total wealth portfolios (including both home and nondomestic assets) and then the US share of the nondomestic portion of the global investor's portfolio.

The home bias of the global investor's equity portfolio (e.g., the share of the equity portfolio that is domestic assets) fell from about 85 percent in 1997 to 75 percent in 2006. During that period, the US share of the total portfolio rose from about 6 to 7 percent. With respect to the global investor's bond portfolio, the home bias fell from about 77 percent in 1997 to about 70 percent in 2006. During that period, the US share of the bond portfolio rose from about 6 to about 11 percent (Bertaut, Kamin, and Thomas 2008, exhibit 9). So exposure to US assets definitely increased as part of the foreign financing of the US current account deficit.

---

7. The data are calculated excluding the US investor. The term "global investor" is used here to mean non-US global investor.

However, when Bertaut, Kamin, and Thomas look at the *US share of the nondomestic* portion of the global investor's portfolio, they find that the US share of nondomestic equities *fell* from 36 percent in 1997 to 30 percent in 2006. The US share of nondomestic bonds rose from 25 percent in 1997 to 38 percent in 2001, where it has remained (Bertaut, Kamin, and Thomas 2008, exhibit 10). These calculations indicate that the global investor is indeed displaying modestly lower home bias for both equity and bonds, which implies a greater *ability* to purchase US assets.

But in fact this trend toward purchasing a greater fraction of nondomestic assets has not been biased toward buying US assets. Does this imply that the global investor is starting to shy away from US assets? It could be so, in that it appears that the global investor has an even greater appetite for non-US assets when he or she invests outside his or her home market. However, it could also be the case that dollar depreciation reduces the value of the dollar component of nondomestic assets while increasing the foreign-currency value of non-US, nondomestic assets. Therefore, it is difficult to tell whether what we observe is a revealed preference for non-US foreign assets or the simple algebra of how exchange rate valuation affects the share of US assets in the global investor's nondomestic portfolio.

Another gauge that foreign investor interest in US assets may have topped out is to look for evidence of a risk premium on US assets following a run-up in foreign purchases. The Curcuru, Dvorak, and Warnock (2007) story of unfavorable timing is not consistent with the story of a risk premium on US assets that develops after substantial increases in holdings of US assets by foreign investors. Moreover, using different data and methods, Bertaut, Kamin, and Thomas (2008) also find little evidence that US interest rates are systematically related to foreign holdings of US assets.[8]

A further gauge that foreign investor interest in US assets might have waned is to look at the composition of foreign assets in the global investor's portfolio: Who is buying those assets, at what price, and what kind of assets? As noted by Lane and Milesi-Ferretti (2007), and Mann and Plück (2006), as well as others, a decomposition of US capital inflows (e.g., foreign purchase of US assets) reveals a movement toward bank debt and foreign official purchases, rather than foreign purchases of equities and bonds. This does suggest that foreign *private* investors have sufficient exposure to the United States in their portfolios and may not want much more at current interest rates and exchange rates.

Finally, as discussed in Mann (2002) and Truman (2005), a depreciating dollar (as one measure of the price of US assets) may be evidence that foreign investors collectively have become sated. That is, a sated foreign investor will not buy any more US assets, which nevertheless are being

---

8. Thus, Cline's assumption (in chapter 2) that a higher NIIP generates a higher interest rate is not consistent with the research findings by these other analysts.

offered, net, into the market via the current account deficit. Under these circumstances of excess supply of US assets, the dollar would tend to depreciate. However, in regression analysis, Bertaut, Kamin, and Thomas (2008) find no evidence of a relationship between the size of the NIIP and the dollar (as neither did Gagnon 1996). On the other hand, episodes of adjustment of large current account deficits are usually associated with currency depreciation, as noted in Freund and Warnock (2007) and Mann (1999).

All told, from the standpoint of sustainability research relevant for projections, this body of analysis points out the challenges of projecting both the level and any change in the desire of foreigners to continue to buy US assets and the type of assets. At a minimum, such projections need to consider the future path of a global investor's home bias as well as financial leverage, along with projections of the growth in the overall size of the global investor's portfolio of wealth.

Projections of the Foreign Willingness to Buy

Facing challenges of raw data and speculative assumptions on home bias and financial leverage (the relationship between financial wealth and GDP), few researchers hazard to project the US share in foreign portfolios, which in fact demands making all the assumptions made in the previous section ("ability to repay") to project the "supply" of US assets to the international capital market. Then, all the caveats of the research outlined above must also be addressed so as to project the size of the global investor's portfolio.

Forging ahead nevertheless, in Mann (2003) I used a simple model of the US current account to project the net "supply" of US assets to the global investor. I calculated historical and projected non-US global wealth based on OECD data, assuming unchanging financial leverage, and experimented with various home bias ratios to project a non-US global investor's wealth portfolio. What did the ratio of the net supply of US assets to this global portfolio of wealth reveal when the initial exercise was undertaken in 2001?

Without any change in the value of the dollar (as of 2001) those calculations revealed that more than 100 percent of the *increase* in the global investor's portfolio would have to have been allocated to US assets. This calculation is with regard to the *marginal* investment by the global investor, not the average share of US assets in the global investor's portfolio of wealth. The calculation of the marginal investment in excess of 100 percent strongly suggested a "too high" increase in the supply of US assets relative to the increase in the global investors' portfolio. Thus, the foreign "willingness to buy" was the blade of the scissors that cut in 2001, and the dollar depreciated as foreign investors chose not to allocate more than 100 percent of the increase in their wealth to the US assets that were being offered.

Figure 3.4 Projected share of US assets in global investor portfolio, 2004–20

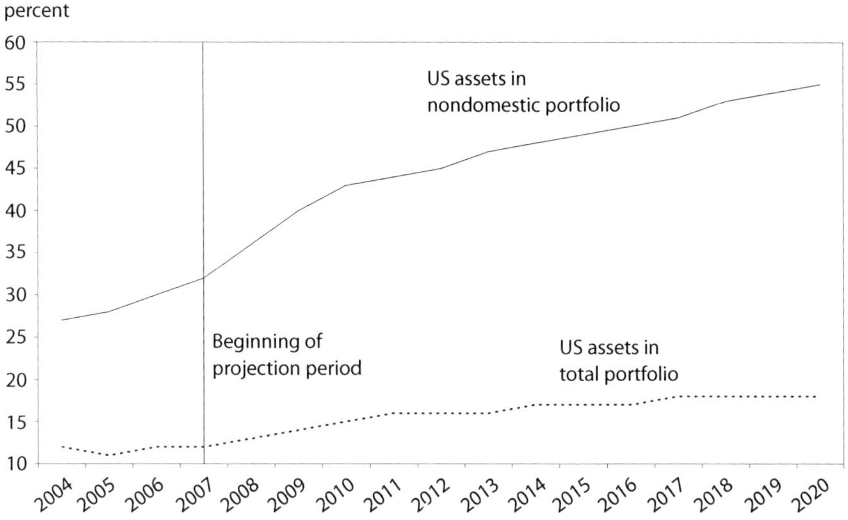

percent

Source: Bertaut, Kamin, and Thomas (2008).

Since 2001, new data have become available on foreign investment portfolios. Bertaut, Kamin, and Thomas (2008) engage in an exercise similar to mine but using these new data. Even with better raw data, they still need to make important assumptions about financial deepening (they assume an unchanged ratio of GDP to market capitalization) and about the composition of the global investor's portfolio (they assume that the bond and equity shares are unchanged from 2007 shares).

Based on their assumptions and their model of the US current account, the US share in the global investor's portfolio would rise from between 7 percent (for equities) and 11 percent (for bonds) to about 20 percent by 2020. The US share of the nondomestic part of the global investor's portfolio would increase from about 30 percent to about 55 to 60 percent (Bertaut, Kamin, and Thomas 2008, exhibit 12).

The Bertaut, Kamin, and Thomas method is more sophisticated than mine, but the spirit is quite the same. However, they reach a somewhat different conclusion than I did about sustainability based on foreign willingness to buy. They focus on the *average* share of US assets in the portfolio and conclude that, whereas the increase in US share of the global investor's wealth portfolio is large, even with this increase, the foreign investor would remain underweight US assets compared with global market capitalization. Inspection of their results (presented in figure 3.4) suggests an inflection point with a significant rise in the average share of US assets in the global investor's portfolio in the first years of the projection. Thus, it is possible that the *marginal* demand[9] on the value of the global investor's portfolio, particularly its nondomestic portion, could be "too large."

Research on future sustainability from the perspective of the global investor's "willingness to buy" gives mixed conclusions. Under some scenarios, it appears that this blade of the scissors might be the one that cuts and that precipitates changes in asset prices, particularly the exchange value of the dollar. However, other scenarios are not so clear and suggest that even by this financial criterion, the US trajectory of global imbalances remains sustainable.

The Global Investor and Financing the US Current Account: New Projections

Based on most of the previous research, it appears that a fresh examination of sustainability of the US external balances based on "foreign willingness to buy" may be fruitful. Accordingly, this section first details how I construct the global investor's portfolio and then examines the relationship between the projections of the global investor's portfolio and the financing of the US external deficit under alternative scenarios for the US current account and gross flows of assets and liabilities drawn from chapter 2 by William R. Cline in this Special Report.[10]

Constructing Projections of the Global Investor's Portfolio

We must start with a projection of the global investor's portfolio, which will be the denominator of the calculation of the share of US assets in that portfolio. Building the global investor's portfolio starts with the historical data constructed by Bertaut, Kamin, and Thomas (2008). These data are more up-to-date, are more inclusive of asset types, and cover more countries than the OECD data I used in Mann (2003). The data available include the global investor's equity portfolio, his or her bond portfolio, and the nondomestic share of each. Using these data one can construct "financial leverage" (total portfolio/GDP, bond/GDP, equity/GDP) and also consider "home bias" (nondomestic share/total portfolio, by equity or bond type). Changes in financial leverage and home bias could be important factors underpinning sustainability because both affect the magnitude of the global investor's portfolio of wealth.

---

9. By marginal demand, the calculation is the change in US assets offered relative to the change in size of global investor portfolio.

10. The projections for the US current account derive from the Cline baseline as of November 2008. He subsequently revised the baselines in light of the larger projected fiscal deficits on account of both the stimulus package and the recession (see chapter 2).

Table 3.1   The global investor's portfolio, 2006

Portfolio	Bertaut, Kamin, and Thomas (2008) (trillions of dollars)	Home bias (percent)	US assets held abroad, Bureau of Economic Analysis (trillions of dollars)
Total portfolio	57.60		
Equity	26.80	75.7	
Domestic	20.30		
Nondomestic	6.50		
of which: United States	1.97		2.55
Bonds	30.76	69.4	
Domestic	21.36		
Nondomestic	9.40		
of which: United States	3.45		5.56

Sources: Bertaut, Kamin, and Thomas (2008); Bureau of Economic Analysis, U.S. Net International Investment Position at Yearend 2007, table 1 on International Investment Position of the United States at Yearend, 2006 and 2007 (line 39 for equity and lines 28, 36, and 38 for bonds); author's calculations.

According to Bertaut, Kamin, and Thomas (2008), the global investor's portfolio was valued at about $57 trillion in 2006 (table 3.1). Non-US GDP was about $35 trillion. Thus financial leverage was about 1.6. In comparison, using a completely different dataset, in Mann (2003) I calculated global financial leverage at 1.7 in 2001 and 1.88 if only the OECD countries were considered. With the broader country group included in the Bertaut, Kamin, and Thomas data, the financial leverage ratio they calculate of 1.6 is probably about right. If the portfolio is decomposed into equity and bonds, the equity financial leverage is around 0.75 and the bond financial leverage is about 0.85.

With financial deepening around the globe, financial leverage in individual countries, and accordingly for the world, might be expected to rise. For example, Bertaut, Kamin, and Thomas's data suggest that financial leverage, as defined here, rose from 1.57 in 2004 to 1.68 in 2006. On the other hand, dramatic upheavals in the financial markets in 2007 and particularly 2008 might cause financial leverage to fall, as consumers keep more of their funds in simple deposit environments rather than equities and bonds. Therefore, changes in financial leverage could change the size of the global investor's wealth portfolio that could be allocated to US assets.

The data from Bertaut, Kamin, and Thomas (2008) also allow calculation of a bond and equity home bias. The home bias is about 0.75 for equity and 0.70 for bonds. I generated about the same home bias for

2001 in Mann (2003). The data for 2004 to 2006 indicate that home bias has been decreasing modestly for both equity and bonds. (As noted, however, just because home bias falls does not guarantee that more US assets are purchased, but it does allow for a greater potential for US assets to be added to the global investor's portfolio. That is, lower home bias points to a larger amount of investable wealth directed toward nondomestic assets, some of which can be US assets.) Table 3.1 shows the decomposition of the global investor's portfolio according to the Bertaut, Kamin, and Thomas data, by domestic and nondomestic assets, including US assets.

Whereas home bias has generally been falling, the share of US assets in the global investor's portfolio, as noted in the previous section, has remained stable (bonds) or fallen (equity). Financial upheaval might lead to a retrenchment toward domestic assets, perhaps reducing the share of the global investor's pie that would be available to purchase US assets. Conversely, financial upheaval could lead to flight to quality international assets, which historically at least have been US assets (and indeed this has been the case as the financial crisis unfolded in September 2008). Thus both home bias and the share of US assets in the portfolio could change over time.

Reconciling Financial Data for the Base Period

The scenarios of how the share of US assets in the global portfolio of wealth might change require projecting both the "numerator" (US assets sold abroad) and a "denominator" (the global investor's portfolio). The numerator of the calculation is based on the November 2008 projections by Cline, the update of which is in chapter 2. The denominator is based on the Bertaut, Kamin, and Thomas data, which must be adjusted to be consistent with the Cline projections as discussed below.

The Bertaut, Kamin, and Thomas data (the denominator) are constructed from a variety of sources including the IMF Coordinated Portfolio Investment Surveys and other balance sheet data. However, there is another source of data on US assets held abroad: the Bureau of Economic Analysis (BEA) net investment position accounts, shown in the BEA column in table 3.1. The figures for US assets held abroad according to the two datasets do not match—they are not even close. While a full discussion of why the two are so dissimilar is beyond the scope of this chapter, the differences must be reconciled because the projections of US assets held abroad (numerator) are based on the BEA data and decomposition whereas the global portfolio (denominator) is based on the sources used by Bertaut, Kamin, and Thomas (2008). Therefore, an adjustment must be made to make the two datasets comparable for the overlap year of 2006 so that the numerator and denominator start on a comparable basis.

There are two ways to make the two datasets comparable in 2006 and hold that comparison constant through the projection period. Either the ratio of the two datasets or the *level difference* between the two datasets in

2006 can be held constant. I chose to hold the level difference between the two datasets constant so as to preserve the trajectory of the projections based on the November 2008 Cline scenarios.

Modeling Portfolio Growth

The final piece of the puzzle is the underlying fundamentals of portfolio growth, which are assumed to equal non-US world GDP growth, which is taken from the Cline projections and adjusted for financial leverage. Later these two assumptions will be adjusted. The baseline growth of the global investor's portfolio is assumed to be:

Total Portfolio(t+1) = Total Portfolio(t) + (GDP(t–1) – GDP(t))*financial leverage

To generate total financial wealth of the global investor, each dollar growth of nominal non-US world GDP is assumed to expand by the financial leverage parameter. This allows examination of how the US share in the global investor's portfolio changes with different assumptions about the growth of the portfolio through GDP growth, through financial leverage, and, potentially, through home bias.

Baseline Global Wealth: Global Investor Average Shares

Figure 3.5 shows the trajectory for the share of US assets in the global investor's total portfolio using the November 2008 Cline scenarios: baseline, sim1 (bond rate rises due to NIIP), sim2 (fiscal erosion, rising bond rate due to fiscal deficit, but not NIIP, dollar depreciates, then appreciates), and sim3 (fiscal erosion, rising bond rate due to NIIP and fiscal deficit, dollar depreciates, then appreciates). (Figures in appendix 3A show the trajectory for the bond rate, the exchange value of the dollar, and price—factors important to the evolution of US assets held abroad.)

In the first scenarios, the baseline and sim1 (higher bond rate) yield a rising share of US assets in the global investor's portfolio. But by the end of the projection horizon in 2030, the US share of the total portfolio is between 20 and 25 percent—about a doubling of the current share of US assets in the total portfolio. This is similar to the Bertaut, Kamin, and Thomas (2008) scenario, which, as they note, leaves the US asset share below a reasonable weight based on market capitalization. So neither the baseline scenario nor one with higher interest rates alone appears to yield concerns about the foreign willingness to buy, although the US share of the portfolio does rise beyond what it has been in the past.

On the other hand, the fiscal erosion scenarios (sim2 and sim3) yield a US share of the global investor's portfolio rising to between 30 and 37 percent by the end of 2030. These shares are higher because higher bond yields (due to fiscal erosion in sim2) and even further increases in bond yields due to rising negative NIIP (in sim3) worsen the current

Figure 3.5   US bonds and equities: Share of global wealth portfolio, 2008–30

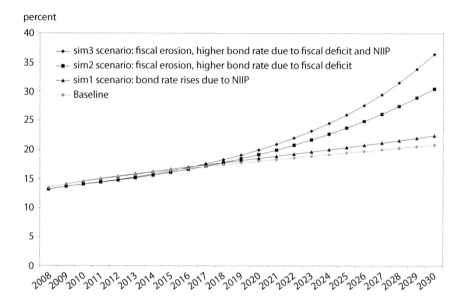

percent

Legend:
- sim3 scenario: fiscal erosion, higher bond rate due to fiscal deficit and NIIP
- sim2 scenario: fiscal erosion, higher bond rate due to fiscal deficit
- sim1 scenario: bond rate rises due to NIIP
- Baseline

NIIP = net international investment position

account deficit via higher net investment income payments, which then require additional US assets to be sold abroad.

Is 30 or 37 percent too high a share of US assets in the global investor's portfolio? Based on market capitalization (US market cap versus global market cap), these percentages would appear to imply US assets in the global investor's portfolio about equal to the market cap weights. Bertaut, Kamin, and Thomas note that historically the global investor has been underweight US assets. By that reasoning, global investors in the fiscal erosion scenarios would just be buying and holding what they "should" of US assets. The United States would be paying an interest premium to the foreigners to induce them to hold the assets. But, at 30 to 37 percent, the US share of the total portfolio would be larger than the nondomestic share of the global portfolio in 2006. So the global investor would have to be moving significantly away from holding his or her own domestic assets or any foreign asset other than US assets.

Baseline Global Wealth: Global Investor Marginal Shares

However, I noted another perspective in Mann (2003): It was not the *average* share in the portfolio of wealth that mattered for sustainability so much as

Figure 3.6   US bonds and equities: Share of change in global wealth portfolio, 2008–30

percent

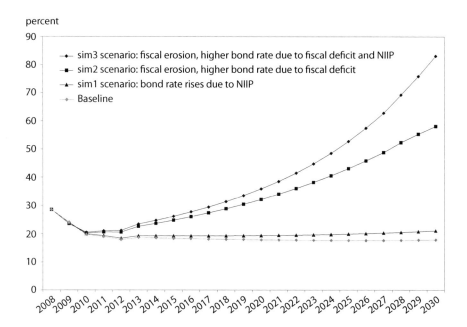

the *marginal* investment requirement. That is, it was the flow of US assets relative to the change in the global investor's portfolio that breached 100 percent—implying that every $1 increase in the global investor's portfolio had to be invested in US assets.

Figure 3.6 shows the calculations for this *marginal* investment requirement. For both the baseline and sim1 (bond rate rising), the marginal demand on the global investor's portfolio stays just at the 20 percent rate, consistent with the 20 percent average share reached in the first scenario. During the period 2009–13 or so, the current account is improving (due to lagged effects of dollar devaluation), so the flow of US assets abroad is not rising. In these two simulations, over the whole of the projection period, the marginal demand on the global investor's portfolio is about the average—there appear to be no problems with sustainability.

However, for the fiscal erosion scenarios (sim2 and sim3), once the lagged effect of the depreciation of the dollar on valuation erodes and the dollar starts to appreciate (due to higher relative returns), the marginal demand on the global investor's portfolio starts to increase dramatically. By the middle of the projection period (2018) the marginal US share of foreign wealth is at current average market capitalization of 30 percent. Anything above this 30 percent would indicate foreigners moving more and more of the increase in their portfolios into US assets. By the end of the projection, the global investor has to put 60 cents (sim2) or 85 cents (sim3) of each $1 increase in his or her portfolio into US assets. This looks unreasonable! It implies a shift away from "home" bias toward "US asset" bias. Therefore, as with Mann (2003), it is not so much the average investment that might drive an unsustainable situation but rather the marginal demand on the global investor's portfolio.

Baseline Global Wealth: Global Investor Purchases of Bonds Only—Marginal and Average Shares

The point about the difference between portfolio investment on average and investment of the marginal increase in the portfolio is even more abundantly clear when just the projections for the bond portfolio are considered. As it turns out, the Cline projections for changes in US assets held abroad channel only through the bond portion of the portfolio. His projections for FDI and US equity held abroad do not change across the various simulations. This, it could be argued, is consistent with the fiscal erosion scenario, whereby the US government must issue an increasing amount of US bonds. Therefore, the demand on the global investor's *bond* portfolio might be most vulnerable. Figure 3.7 shows both the average and marginal investment of US bonds in the global investor's bond portfolio under the Cline baseline and sim3 (fiscal erosion, bond rate rises) scenarios.

Under the baseline scenario, neither the average nor the marginal investment in bonds seems too unreasonable—in fact, there seems to be little pressure on the global investor's portfolio allocation to change from its current allocation.

On the other hand, consider the most extreme fiscal erosion scenario where bond rates rise on account of fiscal erosion and NIIP (sim3). The average share of US bonds in the portfolio seems manageable (and perhaps desired given the assumed higher yield on the US bonds), with the average share rising to 60 cents of each dollar in the global investor's portfolio. Recall that the Bertaut, Kamin, and Thomas (2008) analysis found that the share of US bonds in bond market capitalization ranged from about 40 to 45 percent. This benchmark is breached, in terms of average share in the global portfolio, in about 2024 for the most extreme sim3 scenario; 2024 is a long way off.

However, if we consider the *marginal* demand on the global investor's bond portfolio, by 2025, 100 percent of each $1 increase in global wealth must be allocated to US bonds. More potently, the marginal demand breaches the maximum historical average holding in about 2014 in the extreme sim3 scenario. Put differently, if foreign investors keep to their historical pattern of holding US bonds in their portfolio, the US current account becomes financially unsustainable in 2014 because at that point,

Figure 3.7   US bond assets: Share of global bond portfolio and share of change in global bond portfolio, 2008–30

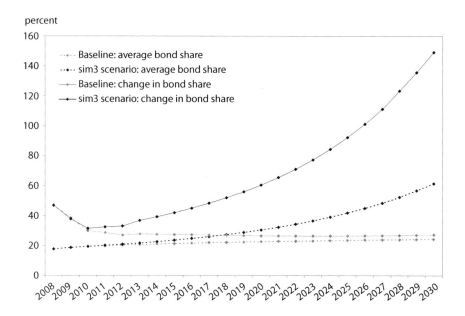

percent

- ⋯⋯ Baseline: average bond share
- ⋯•⋯ sim3 scenario: average bond share
- —•— Baseline: change in bond share
- —▲— sim3 scenario: change in bond share

more than 40 cents of each $1 increase in the foreign investor's bond portfolio must be allocated to US bonds.

Alternative Scenarios for Global Wealth: Slower Growth and Lower Financial Leverage

It is useful to do a sensitivity analysis on these projections. The most obvious issue is whether the global portfolio of wealth will grow as fast as assumed.[11] Two key ingredients are non-US GDP growth and financial leverage, or the extent to which each dollar of GDP growth is magnified into a growing wealth portfolio. A change in home bias is a third way in which to vary these scenarios but yields no new insights. Figure 3.8 (for the average share) and figure 3.9 (for the marginal investment) present sensitivity analysis along these two parameters for the total wealth portfolio.

- ▪ *Slower global growth*: The non-US rate of GDP growth is held 1 percentage point less than that assumed by Cline in November 2008. This assumption is for the financial side only and does not consider

---

11. Given the precipitous decline in global growth rates between November 2008 and April 2009, even the slow-growth assumptions used here likely overstate global growth.

Figure 3.8 US bonds and equities, alternative scenarios: Share of global wealth portfolio, 2008–30

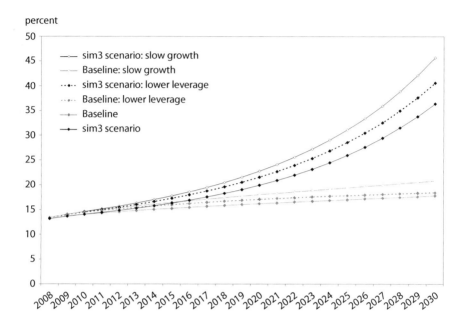

Figure 3.9 US bonds and equities, alternative scenarios: Share of change in global wealth portfolio, 2008–30

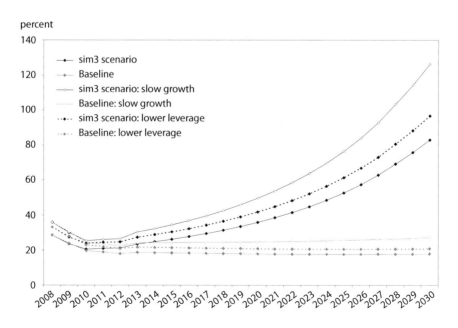

the impact of slower growth on US exports and the current account. Therefore, this assumption supports a relatively benign trajectory for the US current account.

■ *Lower financial leverage*: The financial leverage parameter is assumed to fall from 1.6 to 1.4. This might be related to a deleveraging of the global financial system away from bonds and equity towards bank loans and deposits in response to recent stresses.

The bottom line from these alternative scenarios is that under the baseline scenario, even slower non-US global GDP growth and financial deleveraging do not appear to generate financially unsustainable conditions. In terms of both average share and marginal investment, the numbers for how much the global investor "needs" to buy US assets remain around historical norms—in the 20 to 30 percent range.

On the other hand, the situation in the most severe fiscal erosion scenario (sim3) is made worse by both slower global growth and deleveraging because both of these situations reduce the growth in the global investor's portfolio of wealth. Comparing the two alternative assumptions, the prospects for a financially unsustainable US current account deficit hinges more on growth prospects than on financial deleveraging. That is, the scenarios are quite sensitive to a 1 percentage point reduction in nominal non-US global growth (a reduction in global growth, which is quite plausible). The scenarios are less sensitive to the assumed financial deleveraging from 1.6 to 1.4 (which is much lower than historical experience).

Considering just the bond financing (not shown), the fiscal erosion scenarios combined with slower global GDP growth and commensurate slower growth of global investable wealth immediately breach historical parameters of the bond component of the financing of the US current account deficit. By 2016, even switching from bond to equity financing puts the financial picture under stress. In sum, the combination of fiscal erosion, slower growth, and financial deleveraging would appear to yield near immediate financial unsustainability unless foreign investors alter substantially their preferences toward holding US assets, particularly bonds.[12]

Conclusion

International financial theory points to two analytical approaches to modeling financial sustainability: Is an external deficit unsustainable because a country is unable to make good on (e.g., repay with interest) its previously incurred liabilities or because foreign investors are unwilling

---

12. This indeed has occurred during the early part of 2009 but, depending on a near permanent "flight to risk-free US assets," it is probably also not sustainable.

to buy the assets that are being offered in the global marketplace because they have enough already? The essence of sustainability research is to undertake projections of the US external deficit and consider both analytical propositions to see in which situation the United States appears most vulnerable.

Challenges face those who do projections for either analytical proposition. On the side of "ability to repay" the biggest challenges are valuation effects and rate-of-return differentials, which can make or break conclusions with regard to the size of the NIIP, the magnitude of net investment income, and therefore the sustainability of the US current account deficit as judged from this US-centric perspective. On balance, previous researchers find that if valuation effects and the FDI premium are observed in the future more or less as they have been in the past, the US-centric "ability to pay" criterion for sustainability is not likely to be the source of financial vulnerability until well out in any projection horizon—that is, beyond 2020. Only radical assumptions of no valuation effects and complete erosion of the FDI premium lead to the conclusion that the United States likely would be unable or unwilling to make good on its obligations.

The main challenge facing those who assess sustainability from the point of view of the global investor is how to value and project the global investor's portfolio. At a minimum, such projections need to consider the future path of the global portfolio of wealth, which includes GDP growth, financial leverage, and home bias. Previous research suggests that the inconsistency between the growth of the global investor's portfolio and the supply of US assets in the global marketplace was one source of financial vulnerability in 2001 and was associated with the timing of the dollar depreciation then.

This chapter has considered new projections of the US current account and of global investable wealth to address the question of financial vulnerability in light of the potential for significant erosion of the fiscal budget in the United States.

Under the baseline scenario, neither the average nor the marginal purchase of US assets by the global investor seems too unreasonable—in fact, there seems to be little pressure on the global investor's portfolio allocation to change from its current allocation.

On the other hand, in the most extreme fiscal erosion scenario (sim3— fiscal deficit, larger NIIP, and higher bond rates for both reasons) quite quickly after the initial valuation effects of dollar depreciation wear off (2013 or so), the marginal demand on the global investor's portfolio to be allocated to US bonds breaches the maximum historical average of 45 percent in about 2014. Thus, if foreign investors keep to their historical pattern of holding US bonds in their portfolio, the US current account becomes financially unsustainable in just a few years.

Alternative scenarios for a slower-growing global wealth portfolio, including from slower non-US global GDP growth and financial deleveraging, make it more difficult for the United States to finance the current account deficit, but only in the case of the fiscal erosion scenarios. Prospects for an unsustainable US deficit hinge more on foreign growth prospects than on financial deleveraging. The very real prospects for slower global growth and financial deleveraging, combined with the very likely significant increase in the fiscal deficit, point to near immediate financial unsustainability.

In considering all the research, the marginal demand on the global investor's portfolio is the best way to look at US financial sustainability. Under the baseline scenario, this marginal demand on the global investor's portfolio remains within historical norms. However, given the fiscal erosion scenarios, US external financing needs could, in just a few years, breach these historical norms. Prospects for slower foreign GDP growth and financial deleveraging, both of which slow the growth in the foreign portfolio of wealth, exacerbate the situation, with a near immediate possibility of financial unsustainability. Whether the global investor demands higher interest rates to purchase US assets or chooses not to purchase US assets and so lets the dollar depreciate remains to be seen.

References

Bertaut, Carol, Steve Kamin, and Charles Thomas. 2008. *How Long Can the Unsustainable US Current Account Be Sustained?* International Finance Discussion Paper 935 (July). Washington: Federal Reserve Board of Governors.

Cline, William R. 2005. *The United States as a Debtor Nation*. Washington: Institute for International Economics and Center for Global Development.

Curcuru, Stephanie E., Charles P. Thomas, and Frank E. Warnock. 2008. Current Account Sustainability and the Relative Reliability of the International Accounts. University of Wisconsin. Photocopy (April).

Curcuru, Stephanie E., Tomas Dvorak, and Francis E. Warnock. 2007. *The Stability of Large External Imbalances: The Role of Returns Differentials*. International Finance Discussion Paper 894 (April). Washington: Federal Reserve Board of Governors.

Freund, Caroline, and Frank E. Warnock. 2007. Current Account Deficits in Industrial Countries: The Bigger They Are the Harder They Fall? In *G7 Current Account Imbalances Sustainability and Adjustment*, ed. Richard H. Clarida. Cambridge, MA: National Bureau of Economic Research and University of Chicago Press.

Gagnon, Joseph E. 1996. *Net Foreign Assets and Equilibrium Exchange Rates: Panel Evidence.* International Finance Discussion Paper 574. Washington: Federal Reserve Board of Governors.

Gourinchas, Pierre-Olivier, and Hélène Rey. 2007. From World Bank to World Venture Capitalist: US External Adjustment and the Exorbitant Privilege. In *G7 Current Account Imbalances Sustainability and Adjustment*, ed. Richard H. Clarida. Cambridge, MA: National Bureau of Economic Research and University of Chicago Press.

Henderson, Dale, and Kenneth Rogoff. 1982. Negative Net Foreign Asset Positions and Stability in a World Portfolio Balance Model. *Journal of International Economics* 13: 85–194.

Higgins, Matthew, Thomas Klitgaard, and Cedric Tille. 2006. *Borrowing Without Debt? Understanding the US International Investment Position*. Federal Reserve Bank of New York Staff Report 271 (December). New York: Federal Reserve Bank of New York.

Higgins, Mathew, Thomas Klitgaard, and Cedric Tille. 2005. The Income Implications of Rising US International Liabilities. *Current Issues in Economics and Finance* 11, no. 12 (December). New York: Federal Reserve Bank of New York.

Lane, Phillip R., and Gian Milesi-Ferretti. 2007. A Global Perspective on External Positions. In *G7 Current Account Imbalances Sustainability and Adjustment*, ed. Richard H. Clarida. Cambridge, MA: National Bureau of Economic Research and University of Chicago Press.

Kitchen, John. 2007. Sharecroppers or Shrewd Capitalists? Projections of the US Current Account, International Income Flows, and Net International Debt. *Review of International Economics* 15, no. 5: 1036–61.

Mann, Catherine L. 1999. *Is the US Trade Deficit Sustainable?* Washington: Institute for International Economics.

Mann, Catherine L. 2002. Perspectives on the US Current Account Deficit and Sustainability. *Journal of Economic Perspectives* 16, no. 3 (Summer): 131–52.

Mann, Catherine L. 2003. *How Long the Strong Dollar?* In *Dollar Overvaluation and the World Economy*, ed. C. Fred Bergsten and John Williamson. Washington: Institute for International Economics.

Mann, Catherine L., and Katharina Plück. 2006. The United States as Net Debtor: How Much Longer the "Exorbitant Privilege"? In *Sharing the Growing Burden of World Order*, ed. Jens van Scherpenberg and Katharina Plück. Berlin: SWP.

Roubini, Nouriel, and Brad Setser. 2004. The US as a Net Debtor: The Sustainability of the US External Imbalances. Photocopy (November).

Truman, Edwin M. 2005. *Postponing Global Adjustment: An Analysis of the Pending Adjustment of Global Imbalance*. Working Paper 05-6. Washington: Institute for International Economics.

Appendix 3A   Relevant variables from the Cline November 2008 projections, 2006–30

Figure 3A.1   Bond rate

percent

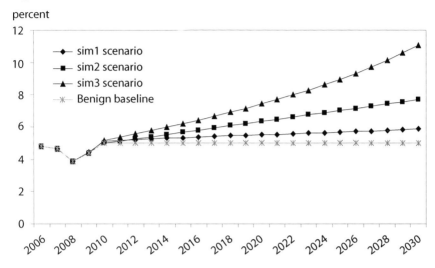

Figure 3A.2   Valuation changes: Prices

billions of dollars

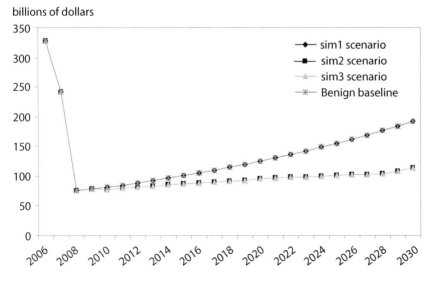

Figure 3A.3   Valuation changes: Exchange rate

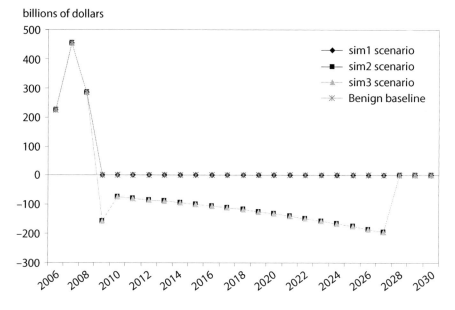

4

National Security Risks from Accumulation of Foreign Debt

ADAM S. POSEN

Every successive year's accumulation of foreign debt (or reduction in the US international investment position) increases the national security risks for the United States. The dollar's global role—in trade, invoicing, and official reserves and investor portfolios—depends critically on the belief that assets held in dollars will not be subject to sustained devaluation. But as foreign indebtedness rises, this perception of the US currency weakens. The United States' political leadership in security, commercial, and even cultural affairs globally has a critical two-way linkage with the faith in the dollar in the monetary realm. When the dollar is believed to have underlying strength, it is to traders' advantage to sign contracts and to price in dollar terms and to trade with countries that also deal in dollars—including the United States—so economic ties between dollar-reliant nations deepen.[1] When the dollar is considered universally liquid and a reliable source of value, regimes that are linked to the United States on foreign policy grounds tend to also peg to the dollar or at least use the dollar as a reference currency.[2]

Adam S. Posen is deputy director of the Peterson Institute for International Economics, where he has been a senior fellow since 1997.

1. In the economics literature, this is referred to as the "endogenous currency area" argument for foreign exchange relationships, as coined by Jeffrey A. Frankel and Andrew K. Rose—i.e., a common currency gives rise to greater trade.

2. Most countries engage in at least managed floating with reference to a specific currency, even if they do not formally peg their currencies, as established by Guillermo A. Calvo and Carmen M. Reinhart's "fear of floating" research. In Posen (2008) I give examples of the interaction between security ties and exchange rate relationships.

This positive economic dynamic that emerges from relative US financial stability has significant benefits for the global role of the United States beyond the monetary or even trade realm. Some of what is taken for granted in foreign policy as the benefits of American military preeminence or political leadership is actually in part attributable, or at least importantly supported by, this economic reinforcement of the US role. This includes many of the "soft power" attributes that the United States enjoys in the cultural and ideological arena, as well as more direct military advantages in terms of access to technology and key geographic areas (and intelligence about them) and ability to encourage bandwagoning with US initiatives rather than balancing behavior by potential allies (in the sense of Stephen M. Walt's [1987] view of alliances) during peacetime or periods of limited conflict. As a result, the erosion of US financial stability through ongoing sizable current account deficits also eats away at US national security.

The Short-Term Risk: Financial Constraint When Responding to Urgent Situations

The usual concern voiced about the national security harms from excessive current account deficits has to do with the risk of dollar-denominated debt being dumped on the market by potential enemies during conflict; occasionally, concern for the accumulation of wealth concentrated in the hands of hostile governments is also expressed.[3] Most national security analysts and financial economists, however, tend to downplay these risks. In times of conflict, the risk is more to the hostile state holders of US debt than to the United States itself, in that fire sales of such debt would amount to the lenders intentionally forgoing part or all of their repayments. The US government would already have (and probably spent) the money lent. In terms of investments in US properties and companies, it is not as though those are transportable to hostile homelands once disputes escalate, as Iran found out in 1979–80. From friendly governments, the threat of such dumping of US government securities is even less credible, especially in times of conflict, when most of the likely large holders of debt (Japan, Germany, Singapore, Saudi Arabia, Taiwan, Korea, and the United Arab Emirates) are militarily dependent upon US security guarantees. If anything, the fact that US hegemony allows the US government to borrow on better terms than any other entity globally should be seen as a privilege (as Charles de Gaulle recognized).

Far more realistic, however, is the national security risk to the United States from current account deficits that emerges when a crisis requiring great public resources occurs during times of relative peace. This could be

---

3. Chinn (2005), Chinn and Steil (2006), Setser (2007), and Bergsten et al. (2008, box 1.2) are all good examples of such discussions.

a military matter, like intervention in Afghanistan, or a broader human security difficulty, like Hurricane Katrina or the Asian tsunami. It could even be the kind of financial crisis in which the United States currently finds itself. In such situations, fiscal expenditures must take a sudden jump. For military interventions or large natural disasters, they usually run in excess of 1 percent of GDP a year for at least two years; for financial crises, the costs are upwards of 5 percent of GDP, sometimes as high as 20 percent of GDP, spread over several years. In all of these cases, demands for US government largesse both at home and from the affected populations abroad go up as well—the United States must be seen as doing its part in leading the effort and the monetary contributions, lest others begin to doubt the benefits of US leadership or even see other countries arise as leaders. Excessive burden sharing is usually counterproductive, not least because it is perceived as an abdication of the US role, leaving the weak and allied in the lurch, if not in danger of outright exploitation.

While the bulk of such temporary surges in expenditure can be financed through US (future) domestic taxes and savings, capital inflows to the US economy can make that financing much easier.

During relatively peaceful times, global capital flows are part of the normal course of economic activity. In fact, the influence of foreign lenders, even those of potential hostile intent, increases during such periods because businesses are willing to depend on such flows and because the selloff of dollar-denominated assets is more credible in such a context (more value will be retained and more viable alternative investments exist).

If the United States essentially maxes out its normal line of credit through excessive and repeated current account deficits during periods without costly crises to which to respond, the terms of US borrowing can erode much more quickly when it goes to the markets for increased bond sales in a short span of time. Moreover, the inflows to US private-sector businesses, for which increases in government funding are an imperfect substitute (as the recent credit crunch amply demonstrates), would be hit even harder if interest rates rise and sentiment turns against dollar investments. Thus not only is there a shortfall in US government resources but also an additional cost to growth in such a period. Finally, if the United States is not seen as a place of relative financial stability, it will not benefit from flight to quality, which usually offsets such problems (again, as seen recently). Hegemony may have its exorbitant privilege, but the United States still is better off saving use of that privilege for when it is really needed. The risk of too much foreign debt is not of being cut off from credit in the true extremis of international conflict but of what happens to American economic performance, relative global standing, and overall resilience when minor but still serious crises occur and US credit is overextended. Too many of such instances mismanaged add up to a long-term erosion of US capabilities and credibility.

The Long-Term and More Important Risk: A Dynamic of Unwinding US Prominence

The positive long-term dynamic that emerges from relative US financial stability begins with the global use of the dollar in trade and investment matters, including as an anchor for other currencies. Such pegging and trade ties orient further the other country's leadership—military, financial, and otherwise—toward US society and politics, be it in public matters of macroeconomic linkages and arms sales or in private decisions about forms of wealth accumulation and where one's children are educated. Private decisions to invest in the United States, both at the corporate level and by individuals, are supported by the desire to gain insider access to key decision-making processes and to membership in US-centered transnational elites; in fact, it is this desire for membership and access that is a major source of the financially unrewarding investments made by foreigners in the United States.[4] Taken together, these many nonfinancial motivations for orienting toward the dollar contribute to the United States' exorbitant privilege to pay for its current account deficits in its own currency at low interest rates.

Yet this mutually reinforcing interaction between currency, trade, investment, and security relationships—which has played out to the United States' national security benefit in countries ranging from South Korea to Saudi Arabia and Panama to Poland—also can go into reverse. Initially, the cumulative nature of these ties means that the United States has more room for error with its currency before things start to unravel, much as the United Kingdom had with the exchange rate ties of its Empire and Commonwealth to the pound persisting even after that nation became a significant foreign debtor. This could explain in part the ability of the dollar to persist in its global role despite the substantial erosion of its net international investment position over the last 40 years. At some point, however, a switch out of the dollar occasioned by the accumulation of too much foreign indebtedness would start to unwind these other ties. Less faith in the dollar would mean fewer contracts and invoices in dollars, lower investment in dollar assets, and diminished trade and financial ties. The elites in the one-time dollar peggers would be economically discouraged from orienting too heavily toward the United States, which could also lead to cultural reorientation and participation in other transnational networks that exclude the United States. And the endogeneity of deepening ties with currency linkages would run in the other direction, away from the dollar.

The distance between the United States' current position and such an unwinding scenario is not all that great and gets closer every year that the

---

4. Charles Maier (2006) and Susan Strange (1996) have made extended historical cases for this process.

dollar's perceived strength is undercut by the country's trade deficit. Given the rise of the eurozone and East Asia as important sources of international trade and global growth, and the substantial role of geographic proximity in determining trade patterns, there is a strong argument for a large number of currencies to peg (or managed float) against the euro, or even the yen or yuan, rather than against the dollar. If undervaluing the exchange rate for export success is important to emerging-market countries, then that is another argument for the targeted currency to shift from the dollar to a basket or to change to a more appropriate anchor as export markets shift.

Indeed, some observers (Bergsten 1997a, 1997b; Portes and Rey 1998) predicted before the euro's launch that the euro would some day rival the dollar as a reserve currency, producing a bipolar monetary system. If the fundamental drivers of reserve currency shares are the relative economic sizes, financial depth, and commitment to low inflation of the dollar and euro economic blocs, then all of these could converge between the United States and eurozone over time, if not eventually, to favor the euro.[5] This economic reality is consistent with financially based calculations of "optimal" reserve shares for countries to hold, which usually suggest the dollar share should be much lower than it currently is. Rather than ascribing this persistence of the dollar's leading role to unspecified "network effects," it makes more sense to view it as the national security bonus from which the dollar currently benefits—and as a marker of just how much economic factors are pushing toward unraveling those ties.

Some analysts (e.g., Bergsten 2005) have argued that for the euro to overcome the inertia of the dollar's role and attain codominance, the United States will have to commit a series of significant policy mistakes or suffer a balance-of-payments crisis. These analysts assume such a process to have been operating when the pound sterling lost its role to the dollar in the 1930s, when the United Kingdom's balance of payments and monetary discipline flagged. The dollar, however, was spared such a fate during the 1970s only because neither the deutsche mark nor the yen was a viable alternative at the time. If the existence of an alternative reserve currency is the key factor, conditional on the basic factors (economic size and financial liquidity) being in place, then recent events indicate that the time is ripe for an accelerated switch from the dollar to the euro, if not a formal regime change.

Such a shift in currency regimes would have significant impact on US national security relationships as well. It is not an accident, for example, that the Central African CFA Franc Zone, where France still intervenes militarily, is the only group of countries outside eurozone membership candidacy to peg to the euro, while EU members with the strongest desire

---

5. Chinn and Frankel (2007) go further and suggest that within 10 years the euro will have displaced the dollar; if the United Kingdom joins the eurozone, adding not just size but also financial depth, this would be accelerated.

for independent security policies (Poland, Sweden, and the United Kingdom) are the ones that have refused to enter the Exchange Rate Mechanism II (ERM II) in preparation for eurozone membership. A wholesale shift to the euro by global investors and official portfolios could possibly tip those countries into deepening their links with the European Union via eurozone membership, thereby starting a cycle turning them from an Atlanticist security orientation toward a more assertive common European foreign policy. And that would be *within* the North Atlantic Treaty Organization (NATO) alliance. Imagine as well the national security impact in East Asia were South Korea, Singapore, and even Taiwan or Japan to feel pushed economically toward deepening ties with China in explicit diversification away from dollar-denominated activities and investments. The impact would be only a little less were such a diversification toward some kind of regional Asian currency arrangement rather than toward the Chinese yuan per se. That would in turn also reduce their educational and cultural linkages to the United States, the volume of transpacific trade, as well as the perceived nonfinancial benefits of holding dollar assets. This dollar decline would not only raise the rate of interest on US obligations but also start a vicious circle of allies distancing themselves from the United States.

In this context, it is worth emphasizing that the main driver in the accumulation of official reserves in this decade has not been the relative reallocation of euros versus dollars. Instead, the big story is the massive accumulation of primarily dollar reserves by Asian developing countries and oil exporters. Developing-country reserves have risen as a share of the global total as their national incomes have risen on the back of export-led growth.[6] This accumulation in East and South Asia is in part motivated by foreign exchange intervention to undervalue these nations' currencies for export promotion and in part to self-insure incumbent governments that they will have sufficient reserves to deter speculative attacks on their currencies of the sort that occurred in 1997–98. In the Persian Gulf, this accumulation has come through inability to sufficiently invest and distribute wealth at home. Whatever the reason, these governments stand to lose the most in financial terms were the dollar to crash or steadily decline in value—these governments are also most on the line geopolitically and in terms of basing for US national security strategy vis-à-vis China and Russia.[7] Thus, the interdependence of the dollar's global role and US

---

6. According to the latest International Monetary Fund's Currency Composition of Official Foreign Exchange Reserves (COFER) data, 75 percent of total developing-country reserves, even counting Japan, are now in official hands. See Truman and Dowson (2008) for discussion of these data.

7. Obviously, Chinese accumulation of dollar reserves is *not* motivated by deepening strategic ties with the United States; one theory does not fit all. At the same time, though, Russia's decision to be the one BRIC (Brazil, Russia, India, China) economy that has openly moved

global security really comes to the forefront today in Asia and the Middle East and underscores the risks to American national interests from current account deficits eroding the dollar's standing, in addition to the direct economic costs.

Since the causality runs both ways from US economic leadership to foreign policy leadership, some seemingly separate aspects of US hegemony will tend to rise or fall together. It is not just that if the United States were to lose reserve currency dominance, military activities would become more difficult to finance—though, of course, they would. Major increases in American foreign indebtedness through current account deficits would also erode the willingness of other countries to deepen ties and networks with the United States and would thus create a negative feedback loop between US economic and security capacities.

References

Alogoskoufis, George, and Richard Portes. 1992. European Monetary Union and International Currencies in a Tripolar World. In *Establishing a Central Bank: Issues in Europe and Lessons from the U.S.*, ed. Matthew Canzoneri, Vittorio Grilli, and Paul Masson. Cambridge: Cambridge University Press.

Bergsten, C. Fred. 1997a. The Dollar and the Euro. *Foreign Affairs* 76, no. 4: 156–80.

Bergsten, C. Fred. 1997b. The Impact of the Euro on Exchange Rates and International Policy Cooperation. In *EMU and the International Monetary System*, ed. Paul Masson, Thomas Krueger, and Bart Turtelboom. Washington: International Monetary Fund.

Bergsten, C. Fred. 2005. The Euro and the Dollar: Toward a "Finance G-2"? In *The Euro at Five: Ready for a Global Role?* ed. Adam Posen. Washington: Institute for International Economics.

Bergsten, C. Fred, Charles Freeman, Nicholas R. Lardy, and Derek J. Mitchell. 2008. *China's Rise: Challenges and Opportunities*. Washington: Peterson Institute for International Economics and Center for Strategic and International Studies.

Calvo, Guillermo A., and Carmen M. Reinhart. 2002. Fear of Floating. *Quarterly Journal of Economics* 107, no. 2: 379–408.

Chinn, Menzie. 2005. *Getting Serious about the Twin Deficits*. Council Special Report 10 (September). New York: Council on Foreign Relations.

Chinn, Menzie, and Jeffrey Frankel. 2007. Will the Euro Eventually Surpass the Dollar? In *G7 Current Account Imbalances: Sustainability and Adjustment*, ed. Richard H. Clarida. Chicago, IL: University of Chicago Press.

Chinn, Menzie, and Benn Steil. 2006. Why the Deficits Matter. *The International Economy* (Summer).

Maier, Charles. 2006. *Among Empires: American Ascendancy and Its Predecessors*. Cambridge, MA: Harvard University Press.

Portes, Richard, and Hélène Rey. 1998. *The Emergence of the Euro as an International Currency*. NBER Working Paper no. 6424 (February). Cambridge, MA: National Bureau of Economic Research.

Posen, Adam S. 2008. Why the Euro Will Not Rival the Dollar. *International Finance* 11, no. 1: 75–100.

---

to a euro-dollar basket for its exchange rate reference is a good illustration of how desire to assert a national security identity independent of the United States can influence currency decisions and reinforce such an orientation.

Setser, Brad. 2007. *The Case for Exchange Rate Flexibility in Oil-Exporting Economies.* Policy Briefs in International Economics 07-8. Washington: Peterson Institute for International Economics.

Strange, Susan. 1996. *The Retreat of the State: The Diffusion of Power in the World Economy.* Cambridge: Cambridge University Press.

Truman, Edwin M., and Douglas Dowson. 2008. Reserve Diversification. Peterson Institute Research, February 5. Photocopy.

Walt, Stephen M. 1987. *Origins of Alliances.* Ithaca, NY: Cornell University Press.

Appendix A

Conference Attendees

C. Fred Bergsten *Presenter*	Director, Peterson Institute for International Economics; Former Assistant Secretary of the Treasury for International Affairs
Joseph L. Bower	Baker Foundation Professor of Business Administration, Harvard Business School
Bill Bradley	Managing Director, Allen & Company, LLC Former US Senator
William R. Cline	Senior Fellow, Peterson Institute for International Economics
Jessica P. Einhorn	Dean, Paul H. Nitze School of Advanced International Studies, Johns Hopkins University
Martin Feldstein	George F. Baker Professor of Economics, Harvard University; Former Chairman, Council of Economic Advisers; President Emeritus, National Bureau of Economic Research
Alan Greenspan	Greenspan Associates LLC; Former Chairman of the Federal Reserve
Robert Greenstein	Executive Director, Center on Budget and Policy Priorities

Peter S. Heller	Senior Adjunct Professor of International Economics, Paul H. Nitze School of Advanced International Studies, Johns Hopkins University Former Deputy Director of the Fiscal Affairs Department, International Monetary Fund
Sebastian Mallaby	Director of the Maurice R. Greenberg Center for Geoeconomic Studies, Paul A. Volcker Senior Fellow for International Economics, and Deputy Director of Studies, Council on Foreign Relations
Catherine L. Mann	Senior Fellow, Peterson Institute for International Economics
Paul O'Neill	Former US Treasury Secretary
Michael Peterson	Vice Chairman, Peter G. Peterson Foundation
Peter G. Peterson *Host*	Chairman, Peter G. Peterson Foundation Senior Chairman, The Blackstone Group
Adam S. Posen	Deputy Director and Senior Fellow, Peterson Institute for International Economics
Robert E. Rubin	Director and Senior Counselor, Citigroup Inc. Former US Treasury Secretary
George P. Shultz	Thomas W. and Susan B. Ford Distinguished Fellow, Hoover Institution, Stanford University Former US Treasury Secretary Former US Secretary of State
George Soros	Chairman, Soros Fund Management
C. Eugene Steuerle	Vice President, Peter G. Peterson Foundation
Paul Volcker	Former Chairman of the Federal Reserve
David Walker *Host*	President and CEO, Peter G. Peterson Foundation Former Comptroller General of the United States

About the Contributors

 **C. Fred Bergsten** has been director of the Peterson Institute for International Economics since its creation in 1981. He has been the most widely quoted think tank economist in the world over the eight-year period 1997–2005. He testifies frequently before Congress and appears often on television. He was ranked 37 in the top 50 "Who Really Moves the Markets?" (Fidelity Investment's *Worth*) and as "one of the ten people who can change your life" in *USA Today.*

He was assistant secretary for international affairs of the US Treasury (1977–81); undersecretary for monetary affairs (1980–81), representing the United States on the G-5 Deputies and in preparing G-7 summits; assistant for international economic affairs to Dr. Henry Kissinger at the National Security Council (1969–71); and senior fellow at the Brookings Institution (1972–76), the Carnegie Endowment for International Peace (1981), and the Council on Foreign Relations (1967–68). He is co-chairman of the Private Sector Advisory Group to the United States–India Trade Policy Forum. He was chairman of the Competitiveness Policy Council, which was created by Congress, throughout its existence from 1991 to 1995; and chairman of the APEC Eminent Persons Group throughout its existence from 1993 to 1995.

He has authored, coauthored, or edited 40 books on international economic issues including *China's Rise: Challenges and Opportunities* (2008), *China: The Balance Sheet—What the World Needs to Know Now about the Emerging Superpower* (2006), *The United States and the World Economy: Foreign Economic Policy for the Next Decade* (2005), *Dollar Adjustment: How Far?*

Against What? (2004), *Dollar Overvaluation and the World Economy* (2003), *No More Bashing: Building a New Japan-United States Economic Relationship* (2001), and *The Dilemmas of the Dollar* (2d ed., 1996).

He has received the Meritorious Honor Award of the Department of State (1965), the Exceptional Service Award of the Treasury Department (1981), and the Legion d'Honneur from the Government of France (1985). He has been named an honorary fellow of the Chinese Academy of Social Sciences (1997). He received MA, MALD, and PhD degrees from the Fletcher School of Law and Diplomacy and a BA magna cum laude and honorary Doctor of Humane Letters from Central Methodist University.

William R. Cline, senior fellow, has been associated with the Peterson Institute for International Economics since its inception in 1981 and holds a joint appointment at the Center for Global Development. During 1996–2001 while on leave from the Institute, he was deputy managing director and chief economist of the Institute of International Finance in Washington.

His publications include *Global Warming and Agriculture: Impact Estimates by Country* (2007), *The United States as a Debtor Nation* (2005), *Trade Policy and Global Poverty* (2004), *Trade and Income Distribution* (1997), *Predicting External Imbalances for the United States and Japan* (1995), *International Debt Reexamined* (1995), *International Economic Policy in the 1990s* (1994), *The Economics of Global Warming* (1992), and *United States External Adjustment and the World Economy* (1989).

Previously he was senior fellow, Brookings Institution (1973–81); deputy director of development and trade research, Office of the Assistant Secretary for International Affairs, US Treasury Department (1971–73); Ford Foundation visiting professor in Brazil (1970–71); and lecturer and assistant professor of economics at Princeton University (1967–70). He graduated summa cum laude from Princeton University in 1963, and received his MA (1964) and PhD (1969) in economics from Yale University.

Catherine L. Mann, senior fellow at the Peterson Institute for International Economics since 1997, is a professor of economics at Brandeis University. Previously, she served as assistant director of the International Finance Division at the Federal Reserve Board of Governors, senior international economist on the President's Council of Economic Advisers at the White House, and adviser to the chief economist at the World Bank.

She focuses on the economic and policy issues of global information, communications, and technology, particularly with reference to the US economy, labor market, and international trade and also studies broader issues of US trade, the sustainability of the current account, and the exchange value of the dollar. Her 1999 book *Is the US Trade Deficit Sustainable?* answers perennial questions about the impact of global integration on the US economy and the dollar. Her chapter "How Long the Strong Dollar?" in *Dollar Overvaluation and the World Economy*, edited by John Williamson and C. Fred Bergsten, addresses concepts of sustainability, including the role of international financial markets and international trade in services. Her other Institute books include *Accelerating the Globalization of America: The Role for Information Technology* (2006) and *Global Electronic Commerce: A Policy Primer* (2000).

On the topics of information technology, trade, and development, she has delivered keynote speeches and engaged in policy projects in China, Thailand, Vietnam, Taiwan, Sri Lanka, Mexico, Morocco, Tunisia, South Africa, as well as in Australia, Canada, Finland, Germany, and New Zealand. Mann taught for 10 years as adjunct professor of management at the Owen School of Management at Vanderbilt University and for two years at the Johns Hopkins School of Advanced International Studies, among other university courses. She received her PhD in economics from the Massachusetts Institute of Technology. Her undergraduate degree is from Harvard University.

Adam S. Posen is deputy director of the Peterson Institute for International Economics, where he has been a senior fellow since 1997. A widely cited expert on monetary policy, he has been a visiting scholar at central banks worldwide, including on multiple occasions at the Federal Reserve Board, the European Central Bank, and the Deutsche Bundesbank. In 2006 he was on sabbatical leave from the Peterson Institute as a Houblon-Norman Senior Fellow at the Bank of England. He has also been a consultant to several US government agencies (including the Departments of State and Treasury and the Council of Economic Advisers), the European Commission, the Japanese Ministry of Economy, Trade, and Industry, and the International Monetary Fund on a variety of economic and foreign policy issues. He is a member of the Panel of Economic Advisers to the Congressional Budget Office for 2007–09.

He is the author of *Restoring Japan's Economic Growth* (1998; Japanese translation, 1999); coauthor with Ben Bernanke et al. of *Inflation Targeting: Lessons from the International Experience* (1999); and editor and part-author of four collected volumes: *The Euro at Ten: The Next Global Currency?* (2009), *The Euro at Five: Ready for a Global Role?* (2005), *The Future of Monetary Policy* (2008), and *The Japanese Financial Crisis and its Parallels with U.S. Experience* (2000; Japanese translation, 2001). He has also published more than

30 papers on monetary and fiscal policy in leading economics journals and academic and central bank conference volumes. He cofounded and chairs the editorial board of the refereed journal *International Finance*. He is a frequent contributor to the opinion page of the *Financial Times* and has also published in *Foreign Affairs*, *New York Times*, *Wall Street Journal*, *Washington Post*, *Die Zeit*, and *Nihon Keizai Shimbun*, among many other leading newspapers.

From 1994 to 1997, he was an economist at the Federal Reserve Bank of New York, where he advised senior management on monetary strategies, the G-7 economic outlook, and European monetary unification. In 1993–94, he was Okun Memorial Fellow in Economic Studies at the Brookings Institution and won the Amex Bank Review Awards Silver Medal for his dissertation research on central bank independence. In 1992–93, he was resident in Germany as a Bosch Foundation Fellow. Posen is a member of the Council on Foreign Relations. He is a research associate of the Center for the Japanese Economy and Business of Columbia University, a fellow of the CESifo Research Network, and has been a Public Policy Fellow at the American Academy in Berlin (2001). He received his PhD and AB (Phi Beta Kappa) from Harvard University, where he was a National Science Foundation Graduate Fellow.

Index

alternative minimum tax (AMT), 19–20
American Recovery and Reinvestment Act, 18
Asia, 70–71. *See also specific countries*

Balanced Budget and Emergency Deficit Control Act, 19
balance-of-payments crisis, national security risks, 69
"benign baseline" scenario, 8, 17, 20, 23, 60–61
   living standards, 31
   long-run prospects, 2–3, 11, 15–16, 34*t*
   modeling portfolio growth, 53–59
   scenario overview and crisis risk, 28
budget deficit. *See also* "fiscal erosion" scenario
   external-sector impact, 16–23
   global investor's portfolio and, 60–61
   implications of current crisis, 6 7
   living standards and, 32
   long-run prospects, 1–4
   scenario overview and crisis risk, 28, 30
   trade deficit relationship, 21–28

capital flows. *See* international capital flows
"capital strike," in "hard landing" scenario, 5
CFA Franc Zone, 69
China, 6, 8, 70, 70*n*
Congressional Budget Office (CBO)

projections, 2–3, 18–20, 19*n*, 20*t*, 23, 28–31. *See also* "benign baseline" scenario; "fiscal erosion" scenario
consumption, reductions in, 25, 30, 32
corporate profits and personal saving, 25, 26*f*, 28
credit bubble, implications of current crisis, 4
credit role, 21
currency pegs, 65, 68–70, 71*n*
currency undervaluations, 8–9. *See also specific currencies*
current account balance
   long-term baseline, 2–3, 11–16
   scenario overview and crisis risk, 28–31
current account deficits, 2*n*, 8, 17, 22–23
   implications of current crisis, 4–8
   international capital flows and, 35–61, 63*f*, 64*f*
   long-run prospects, 1–4
   national security risks, 66–68, 71
   paradox in outlook, 26–28
current law mandate for projections, 18–19, 20*t*, 23*n*

debt service, 2–3, 31
de Gaulle, Charles, 66
demand for dollar assets. *See also* foreign willingness to buy US assets
   long-run prospects, 1–2
   national security risks, 67

projections of, 48–52, 49f, 51f
size and composition of foreign portfolio, 45–48, 46f
France, 69
Freddie Mac, 18, 27

Germany, implications of current crisis, 5n, 6
global capital flows. See international capital flows
global crisis of 2008–09. See also recession of 2008–09
implications of, 4–9
long-run prospects and, 1–4
global investor's portfolio, 3, 60–61. See also demand for dollar assets; foreign willingness to buy US assets
alternative scenarios, 57–59, 58f
average shares, 53–54, 54f, 63f, 64f
constructing projections of, 50–52, 60
marginal shares, 55–56, 55f
modeling portfolio growth, 53–59, 54f, 55f, 57f, 58f, 63f, 64f
purchases of bonds only, 56–57, 57f
reconciling data for the base period, 52–53
size and composition of, 45–48, 46f
terminology use, 46n
gross domestic product (GDP)
budget deficit as percent of, 2, 16–23, 17n, 18n, 23n, 26, 28
corporate profits and personal saving as percent of, 25, 26f
current account deficits as percent of, 1–4, 8, 12–16, 13t, 26–31, 29f, 31n, 37
fiscal expenditure jumps, 67
global investor's portfolio projections, 51, 53, 59–61
national accounts identities, 21
net international liabilities as percent of, 2–3, 12, 15–16, 16n, 30–31
NIIP as percent of, 2–3, 13t, 28–31, 29f, 37–38, 42–43
real GDP decline, 12
tax revenues as percent of, 19

"hard landing" scenario, 4–6, 8
hegemony, national security and, 66–67
home bias
foreign willingness to buy US assets and, 45–48
long-run prospects, 4
modeling portfolio growth, 53, 56–57, 60
new projections, 50–52
US ability to repay, 41–42

household saving. See private saving
housing, 21
implications of current crisis, 4, 5n
long-run prospects, 2
personal saving and, 25, 25n

imports, 21–22. See also domestic demand
long-term current account baseline, 12, 14
paradox in deficits outlook, 26
India, implications of current crisis, 8
inflation, 20
implications of current crisis, 5
long-term current account baseline, 14
interest rates, 20–23, 23n
foreign willingness to buy US assets, 47, 47n
implications of current crisis, 4, 7
living standards and, 32
long-term current account baseline, 2–3, 16, 17f
modeling portfolio growth, 53–54, 60–61
national security risks, 67–68, 70
scenario overview and crisis risk, 28, 30
US ability to repay, 42
international capital flows
current account deficit sustainability and, 35–61, 63f, 64f
national security and, 67
International Monetary Fund (IMF)
data on currency composition of foreign exchange reserves, 70n
coordinated portfolio survey, 46, 52–53
external wealth of nations survey, 41
Iran, national security risks, 66

Japan, 16, 17f, 70, 70n
Jobs and Growth Tax Relief Reconciliation Act (JGTRRA), 18–19

living standards, net external liabilities and, 31–32

mandatory spending, 19
market capitalization
foreign willingness to buy US assets, 45, 46f, 49
modeling portfolio growth, 53–54, 56
Medicaid, 19
Medicare, 19
membership in transnational elites, 68
Middle East, 71
military considerations. See national security risks

national accounts identities, 21–22, 26–28

national saving. *See* public saving
national security risks, 7–8, 65–66
    financial constraint as issue, 65–67
    unwinding US prominence as issue, 68–71
net international investment position (NIIP), 60
    foreign willingness to buy US assets, 47*n*, 48
    long-term current account baseline, 2–3, 16
    measurement of, 38–42
    modeling portfolio growth, 53–54, 56
    scenario overview and crisis risk, 28–31
    US ability to repay, 37–43, 37*n*, 39*f*, 60
net international liabilities, long-term current account baseline, 11–16
net investment income (NII), US ability to repay, 37–38, 37*n*, 42–43, 60
North Atlantic Treaty Organization (NATO), 70

Obama administration, 18–20
Office of Management and Budget (OMB), budget deficit projections, 18
oil prices
    implications of current crisis, 5*n*
    long-run prospects, 1
    long-term current account baseline, 12, 14
    paradox in deficits outlook, 28
oil trade
    long-term current account baseline, 14
    national security risks, 70
Organization for Economic Cooperation and Development (OECD), 45*n*, 48, 50–51
output, implications of current crisis, 5, 32

Persian Gulf, 70
personal saving. *See* private saving
policy considerations, 8–9
    implications of current crisis, 4, 6–8
    long-run prospects, 2
pound sterling, 68, 69
private saving, 2*n*, 8, 21–22, 27
    implications of current crisis, 6
    long-run prospects, 2–4, 2*n*
    revival of, 23–25, 26*f*
    US ability to repay, 44, 44*n*
public dissaving, private saving revival and, 25
public policy. *See* policy considerations
public saving, 2*n*, 6, 21, 27

recession of 2008–09, 17–18. *See also* global crisis of 2008–09
    global investor's portfolio, 52
    long-term current account baseline, 12, 12*n*, 14
    paradox in deficits outlook, 26–28
    personal saving revival, 23
    US ability to repay, 44, 44*n*
regulation of financial markets. *See also* policy considerations
    implications of current crisis, 6
    long-run prospects, 3
Ricardian effect, 21
risk premium, international capital flows and sustainability, 36, 47
risk-return profile, foreign willingness to buy US assets, 44
run on the dollar
    implications of current crisis, 7
    long-run prospects, 3
    scenario overview and crisis risk, 30
Russia, 70–71*n*

safe-haven effect, long-term current account baseline, 12, 14
saving. *See* private saving; public saving
Singapore, 70
Social Security, 19
"soft power" attributes of the United States, 7, 66
South Asia, 70. *See also specific countries*
South Korea, 70
Spain, international imbalances, 5*n*
standards of living, net external liabilities and, 31–32
stimulus program
    contribution to fiscal deficit, 18
    paradox in outlook for fiscal and external deficits, 27
stock market, 12*n*, 21
    personal saving and, 25, 25*n*
    US ability to repay, 41

Taiwan, 70
trade deficit. *See also* current account deficits; exports; imports; "twin deficits" thesis
    fiscal deficit relationship, 21–23, 22*n*
    implications of current crisis, 5–6
    national security risks, 69
    paradox in deficits outlook, 26–27
    scenario overview and crisis risk, 30
transfer of payments, increases in, 27
Treasury securities, 1, 23. *See also* global

investor's portfolio
foreign willingness to buy US assets, 45–47, 46f, 49
global investor's portfolio projections, 50–60, 51t, 54f, 55f, 57f, 58f
implications of current crisis, 7
long-term current account baseline, 14n, 16, 17f
modeling portfolio growth, 63f
Troubled Asset Recovery Program, 18, 27
"twin deficits" thesis, 2, 21

unemployment, 26
United Kingdom, 68, 69, 69n
US ability to repay, 3, 35–38, 59–61
measurement of NIIP and rates of return, 38–42
projections of, 42–44

US asset bias. *See also* demand for dollar assets; foreign willingness to buy US assets
long-run prospects, 4
modeling portfolio growth, 56, 59, 59n
US prominence, national security and, 68–71
US reputation, national security and, 7, 65–66
US Treasury. *See* Treasury *entries*

valuation effects. *See also* dollar valuation
foreign willingness to buy US assets, 47–50
US ability to repay, 38, 39f, 41–44, 60

yen, 69
yuan, 69, 70

Other Publications from the Peterson Institute for International Economics

WORKING PAPERS

BOOKS

IMF Conditionality* John Williamson, editor
1983 ISBN 0-88132-006-4
Trade Policy in the 1980s* William R. Cline, ed.
1983 ISBN 0-88132-031-5
Subsidies in International Trade*
Gary Clyde Hufbauer and Joanna Shelton Erb
1984 ISBN 0-88132-004-8
**International Debt: Systemic Risk and Policy
Response*** William R. Cline
1984 ISBN 0-88132-015-3
**Trade Protection in the United States: 31 Case
Studies*** Gary Clyde Hufbauer, Diane E.
Berliner, and Kimberly Ann Elliott
1986 ISBN 0-88132-040-4
**Toward Renewed Economic Growth in Latin
America*** Bela Balassa, Gerardo M. Bueno,
Pedro Pablo Kuczynski, and Mario Henrique
Simonsen
1986 ISBN 0-88132-045-5
Capital Flight and Third World Debt*
Donald R. Lessard and John Williamson, editors
1987 ISBN 0-88132-053-6
**The Canada-United States Free Trade
Agreement: The Global Impact***
Jeffrey J. Schott and Murray G. Smith, editors
1988 ISBN 0-88132-073-0
**World Agricultural Trade: Building a
Consensus***
William M. Miner and Dale E. Hathaway, editors
1988 ISBN 0-88132-071-3
Japan in the World Economy*
Bela Balassa and Marcus Noland
1988 ISBN 0-88132-041-2
**America in the World Economy: A Strategy
for the 1990s*** C. Fred Bergsten
1988 ISBN 0-88132-089-7
**Managing the Dollar: From the Plaza to the
Louvre*** Yoichi Funabashi
1988, 2d. ed. 1989 ISBN 0-88132-097-8
**United States External Adjustment
and the World Economy*** William R. Cline
May 1989 ISBN 0-88132-048-X
Free Trade Areas and U.S. Trade Policy*
Jeffrey J. Schott, editor
May 1989 ISBN 0-88132-094-3
**Dollar Politics: Exchange Rate Policymaking
in the United States***
I. M. Destler and C. Randall Henning
September 1989 ISBN 0-88132-079-X
**Latin American Adjustment: How Much Has
Happened?*** John Williamson, editor
April 1990 ISBN 0-88132-125-7
**The Future of World Trade in Textiles and
Apparel*** William R. Cline
1987, 2d ed. June 1999 ISBN 0-88132-110-9
**Completing the Uruguay Round: A Results-
Oriented Approach to the GATT Trade
Negotiations*** Jeffrey J. Schott, editor
September 1990 ISBN 0-88132-130-3

**Economic Sanctions Reconsidered (2 volumes)
Economic Sanctions Reconsidered:
Supplemental Case Histories**
Gary Clyde Hufbauer, Jeffrey J. Schott, and
Kimberly Ann Elliott
1985, 2d ed. Dec. 1990 ISBN cloth 0-88132-115-X
ISBN paper 0-88132-105-2
**Economic Sanctions Reconsidered: History
and Current Policy** Gary Clyde Hufbauer,
Jeffrey J. Schott, and Kimberly Ann Elliott
December 1990 ISBN cloth 0-88132-140-0
ISBN paper 0-88132-136-2
**Pacific Basin Developing Countries: Prospects
for Economic Sanctions Reconsidered: History
and Current Policy** Gary Clyde Hufbauer,
Jeffrey J. Schott, and Kimberly Ann Elliott
December 1990 ISBN cloth 0-88132-140-0
ISBN paper 0-88132-136-2
**Pacific Basin Developing Countries: Prospects
for the Future*** Marcus Noland
January 1991 ISBN cloth 0-88132-141-9
ISBN paper 0-88132-081-1
Currency Convertibility in Eastern Europe*
John Williamson, editor
October 1991 ISBN 0-88132-128-1
**International Adjustment and Financing: The
Lessons of 1985-1991*** C. Fred Bergsten, editor
January 1992 ISBN 0-88132-112-5
**North American Free Trade: Issues and
Recommendations***
Gary Clyde Hufbauer and Jeffrey J. Schott
April 1992 ISBN 0-88132-120-6
Narrowing the U.S. Current Account Deficit*
Alan J. Lenz/*June 1992* ISBN 0-88132-103-6
The Economics of Global Warming
William R. Cline/*June 1992* ISBN 0-88132-132-X
**US Taxation of International Income:
Blueprint for Reform** Gary Clyde Hufbauer,
assisted by Joanna M. van Rooij
October 1992 ISBN 0-88132-134-6
**Who's Bashing Whom? Trade Conflict
in High-Technology Industries**
Laura D'Andrea Tyson
November 1992 ISBN 0-88132-106-0
Korea in the World Economy* Il SaKong
January 1993 ISBN 0-88132-183-4
**Pacific Dynamism and the International
Economic System***
C. Fred Bergsten and Marcus Noland, editors
May 1993 ISBN 0-88132-196-6
**Economic Consequences of Soviet
Disintegration*** John Williamson, editor
May 1993 ISBN 0-88132-190-7
**Reconcilable Differences? United States-Japan
Economic Conflict***
C. Fred Bergsten and Marcus Noland
June 1993 ISBN 0-88132-129-X
Does Foreign Exchange Intervention Work?
Kathryn M. Dominguez and Jeffrey A. Frankel
September 1993 ISBN 0-88132-104-4

WORKS IN PROGRESS

Reassessing US Trade Policy: Priorities and Policy Recommendations for the Next Decade
Jeffrey J. Schott

China's Energy Evolution: The Consequences of Powering Growth at Home and Abroad
Daniel H. Rosen and Trevor Houser

China's Exchange Rates: Options and Prescriptions
Morris Goldstein and Nicholas R. Lardy

Global Identity Theft: Economic and Policy Implications
Catherine L. Mann

Growth and Diversification of International Reserves
Edwin M. Truman

Financial Regulation after the Subprime and Credit Crisis
Morris Goldstein

Globalized Venture Capital: Implications for US Entrepreneurship and Innovation
Catherine L. Mann

Forging a Grand Bargain: Expanding Trade and Raising Worker Prosperity
Lori Kletzer, J. David Richardson, and Howard Rosen

East Asian Regionalism and the World Economy
C. Fred Bergsten

The Strategic Implications of China-Taiwan Economic Relations
Nicholas R. Lardy

Reform in a Rich Country: Germany
Adam S. Posen

Second Among Equals: The Middle-Class Kingdoms of India and China
Surjit Bhalla

Global Forces, American Faces: US Economic Globalization at the Grass Roots
J. David Richardson

Financial Crises and the Future of Emerging Markets
William R. Cline

Global Services Outsourcing: The Impact on American Firms and Workers
J. Bradford Jensen, Lori G. Kletzer, and Catherine L. Mann

Policy Reform in Rich Countries
John Williamson, editor

The Impact of Financial Globalization
William R. Cline

Banking System Fragility in Emerging Economies
Morris Goldstein and Philip Turner

The Euro at Ten: The Next Global Currency?
Adam S. Posen and Jean Pisani-Ferry, eds.